The Allotment Gardener's

cookbook

Ann Nicol

Published by SILVERDALE BOOKS
An imprint of Bookmart Ltd
Registered number 2372865
Trading as Bookmart Ltd
Blaby Road
Wigston
Leicester LE18 4SE

© 2006 D&S Books Ltd

D&S Books Ltd
Kerswell,
Parkham Ash, Bideford
Devon, England
EX39 5PR

e-mail us at:-

This edition printed 2006

ISBN 10: 1-845092-93-7
ISBN 13: 9-781-84509-293-1

DS0112. Allotment Gardener's Cookbook

Creative Director: Sarah King
Editor: Anna Southgate
Project Editor: Judith Millidge
Photography: Colin Bowling
Designer: Debbie Fisher & Co

Fonts: New York, Helvetica and Bradley Hand

Printed in Thailand

1 3 5 7 9 10 8 6 4 2

The Allotment Gardener's
cookbook

Contents

introduction

If you are a gardener, you will find growing and harvesting your own produce very satisfying. Whether you have a small or a large garden, a plot of land or an allotment, you will reap the fruits of both spring and summer planting but may find that many of them are in abundance at the same time. From high summer onwards you will be gathering in crops at their peak of ripeness and I hope this book will help you when it comes to cooking or preserving your harvest. You will find advice on the best methods for storing your produce as well as a collection of recipes featuring various fruits and vegetables as ingredients.

If you have a really big glut of a particular item, you will find guidelines on freezing and preserving on the pages that follow. While freezers can deal quickly with bulky stocks of fruit and vegetables, preserving is a much slower process and makes an ideal leisure activity. The pleasure of gathering in the harvest to make jams, jellies and chutneys is timeless and universal. Furthermore, homemade preserves make beautiful gifts for friends and family.

So take a break from the garden and turn your kitchen into a hive of activity. Indulge in baking, and making delicious meals. Fill your freezer to the brim and your pantry with pots of perfect preserves full of colour and texture from the fruits and vegetables you have so lovingly grown in your garden.

Preserving

Preserving is one of the oldest forms of cooking and, for many years, cooks have enjoyed preparing summer fruits and vegetables and preserving them for use throughout the cold days of winter. This is a satisfying activity and many cooks enjoy it as a leisure pastime with a sense of nostalgia for the old-fashioned ways of generations before them.

Jams

The fruit used for jams and jellies has to be cooked before the sugar is added, in order to soften the skin and release an enzyme called pectin, which causes the jam to set. The sugar is added to act as the preservative and to give characteristic sweetness.

Chutneys

For anyone with a productive garden, chutneys are almost as important as jams, because they are a great way of using up poorly shaped fruit and vegetables. Chutney ingredients have to be cooked together to soften them before the sugar is added. Although chutneys and relishes contain sugar they rely on acid, usually in the form of vinegar, to act as the preservative.

Pickles

Pickles need crisp, fresh vegetables, which must first be layered in salt or a brine solution to remove surplus water. Otherwise the water from the vegetables will dilute the pickling vinegar, rendering it too weak to act as a preservative.

Fresh fruits and vegetables

Fruit

Select fruit that is perfect, firm and fresh and not soft or damaged. Slightly underripe fruit is best for preserving, as very ripe fruit has a reduced sugar content, which will affect the setting quality. Sort over fruit carefully and throw out any bruised or damaged pieces. If the fruit needs to be washed, rinse it carefully in cold water in a sieve and dry thoroughly. Try not to wash delicate fruits such as berries. Peel and remove stones immediately before cooking the fruit otherwise the fruit may discolour and deteriorate.

Vegetables

Choose vegetables for pickles and chutneys that are firm but ready for eating. Do not use large or overgrown vegetables as these may be tough and stringy. Wash the vegetables, then peel, chop and prepare just before using.

Sugars

Granulated sugar

This is the cheapest and most easily available sugar and may be used for all preserves. It may cause scum to occur in some delicate jams but this can be reduced by adding a knob of unsalted butter to the jam just before potting.

Preserving sugar

This sugar has larger crystals than granulated and is ideal for making jams, jellies and chutneys from fruits that are high in pectin. The large sugar crystals allow water to enter them easily and this reduces the need for stirring and the risk of burning the base of the pan. Preserving sugar is more expensive but is worth using, as it reduces the scum that can form on preserves, giving a clear bright result.

Jam or pectin sugar

This sugar is ideal to use with fruits that are low in pectin, such as strawberries. The added pectin and citric acid in this sugar ensure a perfect set, while colour, texture and flavour are improved, because the jam does not need prolonged boiling.

Brown sugar

Brown or unrefined sugars give colour and flavour to pickles and chutneys. Molasses and dark muscovado sugars are moist, soft, dark unrefined sugars with a strong pronounced flavour for chutneys. Do not use them for jams, as they will not give a good set and may make sweet preserves become cloudy.

vinegar

Vinegars for preserving must be of good quality and contain at least 5 per cent acetic acid or they will not preserve fruit or vegetables.

Malt vinegar

This has a dark colour and strong flavour and is the most economical all-purpose vinegar for making chutneys and dark pickles.

Spiced vinegar

You can make your own spiced vinegar by heating malt vinegar and adding pickling spices, ginger and bay leaves, or you can buy it ready-made.

Cider vinegar

This is pale, fruity and delicate in flavour. It is a good all-round vinegar and ideal for chutneys.

Distilled clear or white malt vinegar

This is a colourless vinegar preferable for clear pickles and spiced fruits, although the flavour is very strong.

Wine vinegar

This gives a better flavour to more delicate preserves. White wine vinegar is mild and mellow and red wine vinegar adds a delicate red colour, ideal for spiced fruits.

Pectin

A preserve will only set if it contains the right proportions of pectin, acid and sugar. Furthermore, the amount of pectin contained in fruit varies and will affect the setting quality of jams and jellies. Commercial pectin can be added to preserves made from fruits low in pectin to make them set, and is usually sold in liquid form in supermarkets.

High-pectin fruits

Blackcurrants, cooking apples, crab apples, cranberries, damsons, gooseberries, lemons, limes, quinces, redcurrants.

Medium-pectin fruits

Dessert apples, apricots, blueberries, blackberries, greengages, loganberries, mulberries, plums, raspberries.

Low-pectin fruits

Cherries, elderberries, figs, marrows, medlars, melons, nectarines, peaches, rhubarb, strawberries.

Acid

Acids are very important in preserving, as they help jams and jellies to set. They prevent discolouration and improve colour in jams.

Lemon juice:

This is a natural antioxidant and is added to some fruits before cooking to extract pectin and enhance colour.

Citric or tartaric acid:

This can be used in place of lemon juice. For every 1.8kg/4lb fruit allow 2 tablespoons lemon juice or ½ teaspoon citric or tartaric acid.

Salt

Do not use ordinary table salt for preserving, as most brands contain anti-caking agents that will cause cloudiness. Rock salt and preserving salt with larger crystals are pure natural salts and produce the best results.

Spices

Dried whole and ground spices for preserving need to be fresh, or a musty flavour can develop. Whole spices such as cinnamon, cloves, all spice, juniper berries and peppercorns can be tied in a muslin bag and suspended in the pan during cooking. The bag can then be removed easily and discarded.

Dried Fruits

Use good-quality, plump dried fruits for preserving. Rinse dried fruits under cold running water and dry them before use.

Utensils

When making preserves you will need the correct utensils for good results but you will not necessarily need expensive equipment, as many items are already in household use.

Preserving pan or large heavy-based saucepan

This is essential and should be large enough that jam may be boiled hard without boiling over the top, and wide enough to allow the liquid in the pan to evaporate. A preserving pan with a wide base and a looped carrying handle is a good investment if you are planning to make a lot of preserves. Choose a pan made of stainless steel if possible. Copper pans will help keep green fruits green but the metal will spoil the colour of red fruits.

Long-handled wooden spoon

This is vital, as preserves are extremely hot and your hands need to be kept well away from splashes from the jam.

Kitchen scales

Careful weighing is important and the correct proportions of ingredients are necessary for success.

Measuring jugs

Careful measuring of liquids and strained juices can only be done in a marked measuring jug.

Large mixing bowl

This is needed for steeping vegetables in salt or sugar, so choose pyrex or earthenware over metal, which will react with salt and acids.

Jam funnel

This small item makes filling jars an easy and clean process.

Slotted spoon

This is useful for skimming scum from the top of jams and jellies, and for lifting out pips.

Cellophane and waxed discs, elastic bands and labels

These are sold as complete kits in small bags and are necessary for sealing, giving an airtight covering and labelling.

Jars

Used jars must be washed and scrupulously cleaned, dried and sterilised before using. Sets of new jars with screw tops or side clips are ideal for pickles and chutneys.

How to sterilise jars

To sterilise and warm the jars just before you need them for filling with jam, preheat the oven to 140ºC/75ºF/gas mark 1.

1. Wash the jars and bottles in hot soapy water until completely clean. Rinse the jars then plunge them into boiling water.

2. Using a clean cloth, place the jars upside down on a clean baking tray and leave to dry in a warm oven, until all the moisture in the jars has evaporated, for about 20 minutes.

3. Still using the cloth, turn the jars the right way up and keep warm until needed for filling.

How to test for a set

Some preserves will be ready for setting after 5 minutes rapid boiling, but others will need to be boiled for 20 minutes. Make setting tests at 5-minute intervals and when a preserve reaches setting point remove it from the heat at once. If a preserve is boiled for too long, it will never set. There are three ways of testing for a set.

Sheeting or flake test

Dip a chilled spoon into the boiling jam and let the jam drip from the spoon. When the jam no longer falls from the spoon but hangs in solid drips or sheets, the preserve is ready.

Temperature test

If you have a sugar thermometer, dip it in hot water. Stir the preserve and submerge the thermometer bulb completely in the jam. When the thermometer registers 105ºC/220ºF, the preserve is ready for potting.

Plate test

Place a small plate in the freezer for 1 minute. Pour a teaspoon of jam onto the cold plate and let it stand until it is cold. Push the jam with a fingertip. If the jam forms a skin and wrinkles when pushed, it is ready for potting. If not, cook the jam for a further 5 minutes and test again.

Filling the jars

- Fill the hot sterilised jar with jam while it is still hot and in liquid form.
- For preserves with large pieces of fruit or peel in them, leave the jam to settle for 5 minutes to allow the fruit to distribute, otherwise it will float to the surface.
- Fill the jars well. Bring the level up to the top of the neck of the jar as this inhibits the growth of mould. The more air space left at the top of the jar, the more room there is for mould to grow.

Sealing the jam

It is important to seal the hot jam as soon as it is made to keep out air, which contains airborne spores. If these spores are allowed to get in contact with the jam it will begin to develop a mould on top of the surface (see above).

- To seal the jam, wipe the rim of the jar with a clean, damp cloth. Place a waxed disc, wax side down on top of the hot jam. The wax will melt and the paper disc will form a flat neat seal.
- Do not move the jar until the preserve is cold and firmly set.
- Dip a clear cellophane disc in a saucer of water and stretch it over the top of the jar. Secure with a rubber band and leave to dry.
- Cover with a screw top or snap-on lid and label with jam name, month and year.

Labelling

Clearly written labels are needed to identify your preserves and they can be decorative as well as informative. It is a good idea to give each batch of preserves identical labels, so that they can be easily identified. On each label you will need to show:

- The name of the preserve with the main ingredient, for example, 'Strawberry jam'.
- The date of preparation and sealing.
- The eat-by date if the preserve has a short life, or as in the case of pickles and chutneys, the date after which it matures and is ready for eating.

Drying herbs

Herbs should be picked on a dry day, before the herbs have flowered. Snip off any large stalks and discard any damaged leaves from the herb. Plunge into a bowl of cold water and swish around to remove any grit or dirt. Arrange the herbs in small bunches and tie each with a piece of string. Hang upside down to dry in full sunshine, bringing the bunches indoors at night to protect from evening moisture. After 3 to 4 days the herbs should be completely dried. If you cannot dry the herbs in sunshine, place them on a wire rack in a cool oven or an airing cupboard. When the leaves crumble easily the herbs are ready to store. Untie the bunches and rub the leaves off the stalks and store in dry jars or airtight tins in a dry, dark place. Mint, basil, thyme, parsley, oregano, rosemary and bay leaves all dry very successfully in bunches in this way.

Flavoured vinegars

Herb vinegar

Herb vinegars make delicious salad dressings and marinades when combined with olive oil. You will often see them sold in decorative bottles in expensive food halls. To make you own herb vinegars flavoured with tarragon, basil, dill, fennel, chives or rosemary:

- Wash and dry the herbs then pack about 50g/2oz into a 600ml/1pt glass jar. Top with red or white wine vinegar, seal and leave for two weeks, shaking the jar every day.
- Add a few peppercorns, a cinnamon stick or a dried red chilli for extra flavour but these strong flavourings should only be left in the jar for 2 to 3 days.
- Strain the vinegar into bottles and add a sprig of the herb used, then seal.

Raspberry vinegar

Raspberry vinegar is delicious in a dressing drizzled over salads or avocados or can be added to chilled mineral water or soda to make a refreshing summer drink.

- Pick 350g/12oz raspberries when they are very ripe and place in a wide-necked jar. Pour in 1l/1¾pt of red wine vinegar and 2 to 3 thin strips of lemon zest and ½ teaspoon of lemon juice.
- Seal the jars and leave in a cool, dark place to allow the fruit to infuse for 2 to 3 weeks. Turn the jars upside down slowly, once or twice during this time.
- Strain the fruit and vinegar through a very fine sieve, muslin or a jelly bag and squeeze the raspberry flesh through, removing the seeds. Discard the seeds and pour the raspberry vinegar into small clean bottles and label. Seal and store in a cool dark place.

Freezing fruit

Choose only firm, ripe fruits for freezing. If they are soft or slightly overripe, freeze as a purée. Pick over the fruit and discard any damaged or hard fruits. Snip off the stalks or pull out the hulls or cores. If the fruit is dusty or dirty, wash it gently and drain on kitchen paper. If you can avoid it, it is better not to wash soft fruits such as raspberries, as this may cause damage and make the fruits stick together when frozen. There are four basic methods for freezing fruit.

Dry pack

Fruits like red- or blackcurrants, blackberries, raspberries and gooseberries, which do not discolour easily, can be frozen just as they are. Spread the fruit on baking trays lined with cling wrap or non-stick baking paper and place in the freezer until frozen. Pack the solid frozen fruit into strong polythene bags or rigid plastic boxes. The benefit of dry packing is that the fruits will stay separate, so that small amounts can be used as needed.

Dry sugar pack

Soft fruits such as raspberries and blackcurrants can be sprinkled with caster sugar before freezing then, as they defrost, the ice will combine with the sugar to make a syrup. Allow 50g/2oz sugar for each 450g/1lb fruit. Gently mix together, then pack into rigid plastic boxes leaving 2cm/¾in head space to allow for expansion.

Syrup pack

Firm, textured fruits such as apricots or peaches are likely to discolour and are best frozen as slices in a sugar syrup. Dissolve 275g/10oz sugar in 600ml/1pt water, and boil for 3 minutes until thickened. Cool and use 300ml/½pt syrup to pack 450g/1lb fruit. Fruits that discolour such as apples and pears should be tossed in lemon juice to coat the cut edges before adding the cold syrup.

Purées

If the fruit is overripe, purée in a blender or food processor and sieve to remove any large pips or thick skins. Pack into rigid plastic boxes leaving 1cm/½in space for expansion. Use purées to make sweet sauces for ice creams or stir into whipped cream for quick mousse-type desserts.

Sealing and labelling

Try to extract all the air from polythene bags for freezing and seal them with twist ties or freezer tape. Labelling is essential to identify how long the frozen food has been stored. Use a waterproof felt-tip pen or a Chinagraph pencil for labelling so that the information is not rubbed off in the freezer. Polythene bags with a white printed label on them are useful for storage, as the label cannot fall off.

Freezing vegetables

Most vegetables can be frozen, with the exception of salad vegetables like lettuce, cucumber and whole tomatoes. For best results choose young vegetables that have just reached their peak before freezing.

Blanching

Vegetables need to be blanched before freezing to destroy the enzymes present in them that will otherwise cause them to deteriorate. Blanching also helps retain the colour, texture and flavour of vegetables.

- Prepare the vegetables as you would for cooking by trimming into neat pieces or slicing thinly.

- Bring 4l/7pt water to the boil with 2 teaspoons of salt for every 450g/1lb of vegetables. Add the vegetables in a basket if possible, and return to the boil for 1 minute after the vegetables are added.

- Remove the vegetables with a slotted spoon and plunge into a large bowl of iced, cold water to cool the vegetables as quickly as possible. Use new cold water for each batch.

- Drain and toss the vegetables to separate them. For large pieces such as broccoli or cauliflower, spread on a clean tea towel to dry. Pack into plastic bags or boxes, label and freeze immediately.

Methods of preserving fresh fruits and vegetables

Fruit or vegetable	Growing season	Methods of preservation
APPLES (Eating and cooking)	Sept-Oct	Freezing, jam, jelly, chutney
APRICOTS	June-Aug	Freezing, jam
ASPARAGUS	May-June	Freezing
AUBERGINES	Aug-Oct	Freezing, chutney
BEANS, broad	May-Aug	Freezing, drying
BEANS, French & runner	July-Aug	Freezing, pickling
BEETROOT	July-Oct	Freezing, chutney, pickling
BLACKBERRIES	Aug-Oct	Freezing, jam, jelly
BLACKCURRANTS	July-Aug	Freezing, jam, jelly
BROCCOLI, purple	Nov-Dec	Freezing
BROCCOLI, calabrese	July-Aug	Freezing
BRUSSELS SPROUTS	Nov-March	Freezing
CABBAGE, spring	April-May	Freezing, pickling
CABBAGE, summer	June-Oct	Freezing, pickling
CABBAGE, red	Aug-Jan	Freezing, pickling
CARROTS	March-Nov	Freezing
CAULIFLOWERS	Nov-Aug	Freezing, pickling, chutney
CELERY	July-March	Freezing, pickling
CHERRIES	June-July	Freezing, bottling, jam
COURGETTES	Aug-Sept	Freezing, pickling
CUCUMBERS	July-Aug	Pickling
DAMSONS	Aug-Sept	Freezing, jam, jelly, chutney

Methods of preserving fresh fruits and vegetables continued...

Fruit or vegetable	Growing season	Methods of preservation
GOOSEBERRIES	July-Aug	Freezing, jam, jelly, chutney
GREENGAGES	August	Freezing, jam
HERBS	May-Sept	Freezing, drying, jelly
LEEKS	Oct-Feb	Freezing
MARROWS	Aug-Oct	Freezing, jam, chutney
ONIONS	Oct-March	Drying, pickling
PARSNIPS	Oct-March	Freezing
PEAS	July-Aug	Freezing
PEACHES	July-Aug	Freezing, bottling, jam
PEARS	Oct-Dec	Freezing, bottling, chutney, jam
PEPPERS	July-Aug	Freezing, chutney
PLUMS	September	Freezing, jam, chutney, pickling
POTATOES, early	July-Sept	Freezing
POTATOES, main crop	Oct-March	Freezing
RASPBERRIES	July-Aug	Freezing, bottling, jam, jelly
REDCURRANTS	July-Aug	Freezing, jam, jelly
RHUBARB	March-June	Freezing, chutney, jam
STRAWBERRIES	June-July	Jam, freezing
SWEETCORN	Sept-Nov	Freezing, relish
TOMATOES	Aug-Sept	Freezing as sauces, pickling, chutney
TURNIPS	Oct-March	Freezing

Tips for Successful Cooking

- Use metric or imperial measurements only; do not mix the two.
- Use measuring spoons: 1 tsp = 5ml; 1 tbsp = 15ml
- All spoon measurements are level unless otherwise stated.
- All eggs are medium unless otherwise stated.
- Recipes using raw or lightly cooked eggs should not be given to babies, pregnant women, the very old or anyone suffering from or recovering from an illness.
- The cooking times are an approximate guide only. If you are using a fan oven reduce the cooking time according to the manufacturer's instructions.
- Ovens should be preheated to the required temperature.
- Fruits and vegetables should be washed before use.

Servings

Please note most of the recipes have ingredients listed for a number of servings. If the recipe includes servings for two and four people, for example, the recipe will show how much to add for two people, with amount for four people in brackets, for example, 2 tbsp (4 tbsp).

fruit

Apple and Herb Jelly

Perfect preserves

Homemade apple jelly provides a clear base to which herbs can be added, and the vinegar gives a delicious sweet-and-sour flavour. Serve mint or rosemary jelly with lamb, thyme jelly with poultry, sage jelly with pork and parsley jelly with ham.

Ingredients
Makes 1.8kg/4lb

1.8kg/4lb Bramley cooking apples, washed
900ml/1½pt water
2-3 sprigs of fresh herb such as parsley, sage, rosemary or thyme

150ml/¼pt clear malt vinegar
1.51.8kg/3-4lb granulated sugar
3-4 tbsp herbs of choice, such as mint, rosemary, sage or thyme, finely chopped

1 Coarsely chop the apples, cutting away any damaged parts. Place in a large pan or preserving pan and add the water. Tie the herb sprigs together and add to the pan.

2 Simmer gently for about an hour until the apples are very soft and pulpy. Add the vinegar and cook for a further 5 minutes. Spoon the pulp and juices into a large doubled piece of muslin or a jelly bag suspended over a bowl and allow the extract to drip from the fruit for about 8 hours.

3 Measure the juice extract into a jug. Place the juice in a large pan or preserving pan with 450g/1lb sugar for every 600ml/1pt juice. Stir over a low heat until every grain of sugar has dissolved. Bring to the boil and boil rapidly for about 10 minutes then test for a set (see plate test, page 22).

4 Skim any scum from the surface, add the chopped herbs and cool for 5 minutes. Pour into small sterilised, warmed jars (see page 20), stir again to distribute the herbs, cover with waxed discs, wax side down, while the jelly is still hot. Cover and label when cold.

Golden Apple and Honey Squares

Family favourite

If you have a glut of apples, pop them into this quick and versatile tray bake. Serve these sweet apple slices hot with custard or ice cream as a dessert or cold as a cake with whipped cream.

Ingredients
Makes 12 squares

175g/6oz self-raising flour
1 tsp baking powder
A pinch of salt
75g/3oz caster sugar
Finely grated zest of 1 lemon
1 medium egg

6 tbsp milk
2 tbsp vegetable oil
450g/1lb dessert apples,
    peeled, cored and
    thinly sliced
25g/1oz butter, melted
50g/2oz vanilla caster sugar
2 tbsp clear honey, warmed

1 Preheat the oven to 200°C/400°F/gas 6. Grease and line the base and short sides of a 27x18cm/ 11x7in shallow oblong tin with a strip of non-stick baking paper.

2 Sift the flour, baking powder and salt into a bowl and stir in the caster sugar and half the lemon zest. Whisk the egg with the milk and oil and pour into the bowl. Beat together until smooth, and pour into the lined tin.

3 Arrange the apple slices in the batter and brush with the melted butter. Mix the vanilla sugar with the remaining lemon zest and sprinkle over the apples.

4 Bake for 30-35 minutes or until the base has risen and the topping is golden. Cool in the tray for 4 minutes before brushing with warmed honey and cutting into 12 squares.

Tip

To freeze, cool the cake slices without the honey. Freeze, uncut, wrapped in foil. It will keep for 3 months. To use, thaw at room temperature, brush with honey and cut into squares.

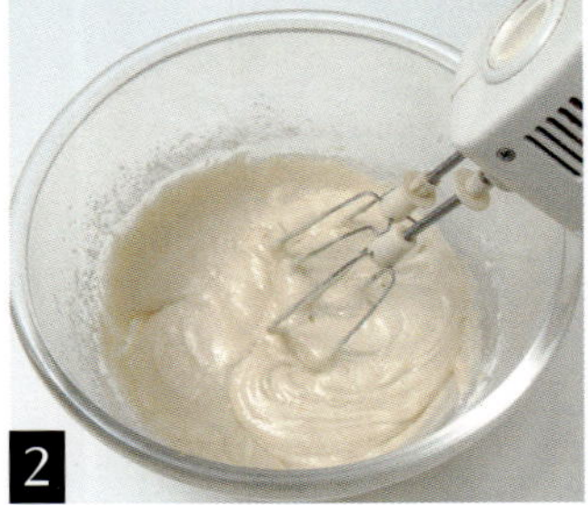

Spicy Apple Chutney

Store-cupboard special

Apples for chutney do not have to be perfect, so use up windfalls or cooking apples that are misshapen. Fresh ginger and chilli are more fiery than dried spices and add a touch of natural heat to this fruity preserve.

Ingredients
Makes 1.8kg/4lb

1kg/2¼lb Bramley cooking
    apples
450ml/¾pt cider vinegar
2 ripe mangoes, peeled
    and chopped
275g/10oz onions, peeled
    and chopped

100g/4oz sultanas
275g/10oz soft, light brown
    sugar
40g/1½oz fresh root ginger,
    peeled and grated
2 cloves garlic, peeled
    and crushed
1 red chilli, finely chopped
1 tsp salt

1 Peel, core and chop the cooking apples roughly. Place in a preserving pan or a large deep saucepan with the vinegar and simmer over a low heat for 10 minutes.

2 Add the remaining ingredients and simmer until the sugar has dissolved. Bring to the boil, stirring continuously.

3 Reduce the heat and simmer for about 40 minutes, stirring occasionally until the mixture has reduced to a thick pulp. Test by running a spoon across the bottom of the pan – you should be able to see the metal base for a few seconds.

4 Ladle into warmed, sterilised jars, seal and label (see pages 20-25). Store in a cool, dark place for 1 month before opening to allow the flavours to mellow.

Tip

Always store preserves away from the light in a cool, dark cupboard or a shelf in a garage or outhouse. Sunlight and heat will make them dry out and will affect both shelf life and keeping qualities.

Apple and Almond Tart

Delicious desserts

Apples and almonds make perfect partners in this easy dessert. You do not even need to roll out the pastry, just press it into place and top with masses of sliced apples.

Ingredients
Makes a 23cm/9in tart

100g/4oz plain flour
50g/2oz butter
25g/1oz ground almonds
25g/1oz whole almonds, chopped
A few drops of almond essence

50g/2oz caster sugar
½ medium egg
700g/1½lb Granny Smith or Cox eating apples
25g/1oz butter, melted
15g/½oz vanilla caster sugar
2 tbsp apricot glaze

1 Preheat the oven to 200°C/400°F/gas 6 and place a baking sheet in the oven to heat. Grease a 23cm/9in loose-base flan tin.

2 Sift the flour into a bowl or food processor, add the fat cut into small pieces and rub in or process until the mixture resembles fine crumbs. Stir the almonds into the mixture with the sugar and essence. Bind together with the egg to make a soft dough and press into the prepared tin.

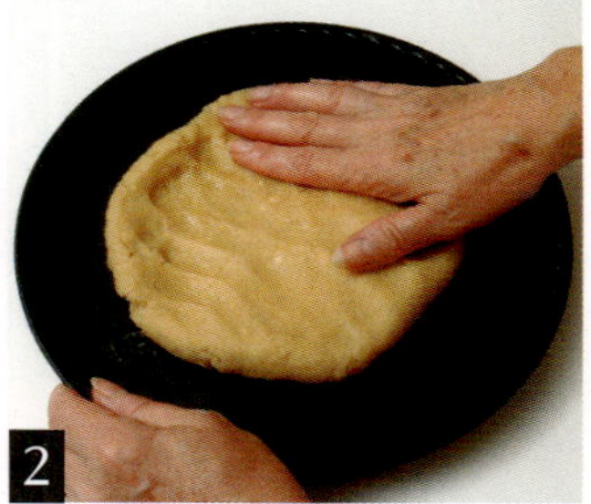

3 Peel, halve and core the apples. Slice the apples thinly and arrange in an overlapping pattern on top of the pastry base.

4 Brush with the melted butter and sprinkle the vanilla sugar over the top. Bake for about 35 minutes until the base is golden and the apples are tender and browned at the edges. Brush with apricot glaze and serve warm or cold with crème fraîche, thick cream or yoghurt.

Tip
Not suitable for freezing.

Fruity Apple Mincemeat

Store-cupboard special

Homemade mincemeat is far superior to the shop-bought variety and is very easy to make. Fill some pretty jars as gifts but keep some stored away to make delicious mince pies at Christmas.

Ingredients
Makes 2.75kg/6lb

1kg/2¼lb Bramley cooking
   apples, washed
225g/8oz vegetable suet
350g/12oz sultanas
225g/8oz raisins
225g/8oz currants
100g/4oz glacé cherries,
   rinsed and halved
100g/4oz dried apricots,
   snipped
100g/4oz chopped mixed peel

50g/2oz slivered almonds
   (optional)
350g/12oz soft, dark
   muscovado sugar
Finely grated zest and juice
   of 1 orange
Finely grated zest and juice
   of 1 lemon
1 tbsp ground mixed spice
½ tsp ground cinnamon
½ tsp freshly grated nutmeg
4-6 tbsp brandy or dark rum

1 Halve the apples. Remove the cores and coarsely chop or grate without peeling. Place in a large mixing bowl.

2 Gradually stir in the suet, dried fruits and nuts, sugar, orange and lemon zest and juice, and the spices.

3 Stir the contents of the bowl well and leave

covered for 3 days in a cool place, stirring frequently.

4 Pack the mincemeat into clean dry jars with stoppers or lidded polythene boxes and spoon 1-2 tbsp brandy or rum over each. Seal with an airtight lid or stopper and store in a cool, dark place for up to six months.

Tip

To use, spoon into pastry cases and bake at 190°C/375°F/ gas mark 5.

Greengage Conserve

Perfect preserves

Bright green greengages are a delicious and delicate summer fruit with a short season, appearing only in the months of July and August. Greengages are marvellous baked in tarts and pastries but you can really capture their wonderful flavour and make the most of a large quantity by making this sweet and tangy preserve.

Ingredients
Makes 3.5kg/7lb 8oz

2kg/4lb greengages, washed
450ml/¾pt water
Juice of ½ lemon
2kg/4lb granulated sugar

1 Cut the greengages in half. Take out the stones and crack them to remove the kernels. Blanch the kernels in boiling water, drain and cut them in half.

2 Put the fruit with the kernels in a large heavy-based pan with the water and simmer until the fruit has softened, about 15-20 minutes.

3 Add the sugar and stir over a very low heat until every single grain has dissolved. Bring to the boil and boil hard until setting point has been reached.

4 Test for a set (see plate test, page 22). When ready, pour into warmed, sterilised jars (see page 20) and leave to stand for 5 minutes. Stir to distribute the pieces of fruit then cover with waxed discs, wax side down. When cold, cover and label.

Tip

If you cannot find greengages use apricots instead, as this recipe is ideal if you have a glut of either fruit. Make sure the fruit is free from blemishes and is ripe but firm.

Apricot and Yoghurt Ice Cream

Easy entertaining

If you are lucky enough to have extra fruits to spare this summer, freeze them in this easy ice cream. The sweet tangy flavour of fresh plump apricots is captured perfectly.

Ingredients for 2

- 350g/12oz fresh apricots, peeled, stoned
- 15g/½oz golden caster sugar
- 1 tbsp clear honey
- 75g/2½oz ready-made dairy custard
- 175g/6oz thick Greek yoghurt
- 375ml/¼pt whipping cream
- ½ tsp vanilla essence

Ingredients for 4

- 700g/1½lb fresh apricots, peeled, stoned
- 25g/1oz golden caster sugar
- 2 tbsp clear honey
- 150g/5oz ready-made dairy custard
- 350g/12oz thick Greek yoghurt
- 300ml/½pt whipping cream
- 1 tsp vanilla essence

1 Place the apricots, sugar and honey in a pan with 3 tbsp (6 tbsp) water and simmer over a low heat until the fruit is tender, about 5 minutes. Leave to cool.

2 Mash or purée the apricots in a processor and mix them with the custard. Fold in the yoghurt. Whip the cream until it forms soft peaks and fold into the mixture with the vanilla essence.

3 Pour into a freezer-proof container and freeze until half-set. Place the half-frozen mixture in a bowl and beat it to break up the ice crystals.

4 Return to the container and freeze again until almost solid. Place in a bowl and beat again until a smooth, half-frozen texture is achieved. Return to the container once more and freeze until solid.

Tip

Remove the box from the freezer and place in the fridge for 30 minutes before serving to allow the ice cream to soften. Serve in scoops with fancy biscuits or ready-made chocolate sauce. It will keep for 3 months in the freezer.

Apricot Mousse

Delicious desserts

These delicate mousses will impress your guests at the end of a dinner party, and yet they are simple to make. If you cannot find the brandy snap baskets, serve the mousse in tall glasses with fancy biscuits instead.

Ingredients for 2

225g/8oz fresh apricots
½ tbsp powdered gelatine
1 tbsp clear honey
1 tbsp peach liqueur or
    fresh orange juice
25g/1oz crème fraîche
50g/2oz thick Greek yoghurt
2 ready-made brandy snap
    baskets, to serve
4 raspberries and 2 fresh
    mint sprigs, to serve

Ingredients for 4

450g/1lb fresh apricots
1 tbsp powdered gelatine
2 tbsp clear honey
2 tbsp peach liqueur or
    fresh orange juice
50g/2oz crème fraîche
100g/4oz thick Greek yoghurt
4 ready-made brandy snap
    baskets, to serve
8 raspberries and 4 fresh
    mint sprigs, to serve

1 In batches, place the apricots in a bowl of boiling water for 1 minute then into a bowl of cold water and slip away the skins. Halve and remove the stones then chop the fruit roughly.

2 Sprinkle the gelatine over 1 tbsp (2 tbsp) water in a small bowl and leave to become spongy. Warm in the microwave on a low setting or in a bowl over a pan of hot water and heat to dissolve. Place the chopped fruit in a processor or liquidiser with the honey and 1 tbsp (2 tbsp) water and process until smooth.

3 Mix the purée with the peach liqueur, crème fraîche and yoghurt and stir until smooth. Stir in the gelatine and mix until well combined.

4 Chill the mixture for about 30 minutes or until half-set. Place the brandy snap baskets on a tray and spoon the mousse into them. Chill for 10 minutes to set and serve each one decorated with 2 fresh raspberries and a sprig of mint.

Apricot and Hazelnut Meringues

Delicious desserts

Make these delicious meringue bases ahead of time, to allow you to concentrate on your main course. Fill them with delicious fresh apricots and cream just before serving.

Ingredients
Makes 6-8

4 whites from medium eggs
225g/8oz golden caster sugar
1 tsp vanilla essence

50g/2oz toasted hazelnuts,
finely chopped
300ml/½pt whipping cream
500g/1lb 2oz fresh apricots

1 Preheat the oven to 140°C/275°F/gas mark 1. Line two baking sheets with non-stick baking paper.

2 In a clean, dry, grease-free bowl, whisk the egg whites until stiff. Add half the sugar and whisk again until thick. Carefully fold in the remaining sugar with the essence and chopped nuts.

3 Spoon dessertspoons of the mixture in rough heaps on each baking sheet. Bake for 50-60 minutes, alternating the trays onto different shelves halfway through. Remove and cool on a wire rack.

4 Whip the cream until stiff. Place a few apricots at a time in boiling water, then into cold, and slip away the skins. Halve each fruit and remove the stone, then chop the apricots finely. Spread one half of each meringue with cream and the other half with the chopped apricots. Sandwich the meringues together just before serving.

Tip

In order to make perfect meringues, the bowl must be spotlessly clean and dry, otherwise the whites will not whisk and hold air. To ensure this, pour boiling water into the bowl to be used, swirl it round and tip away. Dry the bowl with a clean cloth or kitchen paper until every spot of moisture has been removed.

Apricot and Lamb Tagine with Couscous

Easy entertaining

The tartness of fresh apricots complements tender lamb in this fragrant braised supper dish. Couscous is a light fluffy grain, popular in Mediterranean countries, and is often served with meat dishes combined with fruits.

Ingredients for 2

350g/12oz lamb fillet
1 tbsp sunflower oil
1 medium onion, peeled
   and sliced
1 small clove garlic, peeled
   and chopped
½ red pepper, seeded
   and chopped
½ tsp ground allspice
A small pinch of chilli
   powder
½ cinnamon stick
1 tsp plain flour
1 tsp clear honey
1 tsp tomato purée
225ml/8fl oz lamb or
   vegetable stock
Finely grated zest and juice
   of ½ orange
225g/8oz ripe apricots,
   halved and stoned

Ingredients for 4

700g/1lb 8oz lamb fillet
2 tbsp sunflower oil
1 large onion, peeled
   and sliced
1 clove garlic, peeled
   and chopped
1 red pepper, seeded
   and chopped
1 tsp ground allspice
A pinch of chilli powder
1 cinnamon stick
1 tbsp plain flour
1 tbsp clear honey
1 tbsp tomato purée
450ml/¾pt lamb or vegetable
   stock
Finely grated zest and juice
   of 1 orange
450g/1lb ripe apricots,
   halved and stoned

To serve

100ml/3½fl oz water
A pinch of salt
1 tsp sunflower oil
50g/2oz couscous
12g/½oz butter
1 tsp coriander or mint,
   chopped

To serve

200ml/7fl oz water
½ tsp salt
2 tsp sunflower oil
100g/4oz couscous
25g/1oz butter
1 tbsp coriander or mint,
   chopped

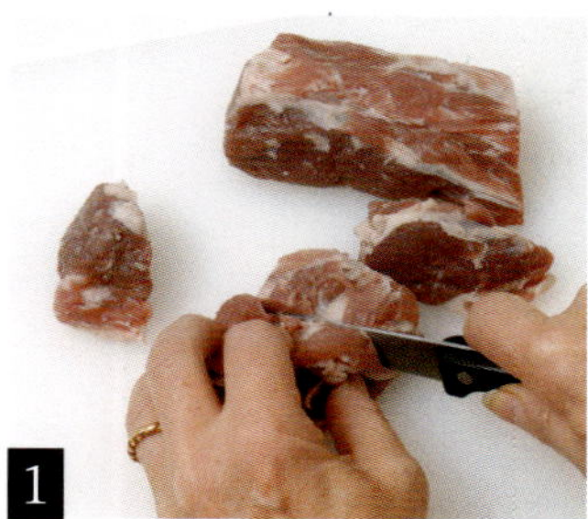

1 Preheat the oven to 180°C/350°F/gas mark 4. Cut the lamb fillet into large chunks. Heat the oil in a large pan and fry the lamb for 2-3 minutes until browned all over. Place in a heatproof casserole and keep warm.

2 Place the onion, garlic and pepper in the pan and fry until softened for 2-3 minutes. Add the spices, stir, and fry for 1 minute. Stir in the flour, cook for a minute then add the honey, tomato purée, stock and orange zest and juice.

3 Pour into the casserole dish with the lamb, cover with a lid or foil and cook for 1 hour. Add half the apricots and cook for a further 20 minutes until they have softened.

4 Make the couscous. Place the water in a saucepan, add the salt and oil and heat gently. Stir in the couscous with a wooden spoon. Cover and remove from the heat for 3 minutes until the water has been nearly absorbed. Add the butter and return to the heat. Cook gently, for 3-4 minutes. Place in a bowl and separate the grains before serving. Garnish with chopped herbs and the remaining chopped fresh apricots.

Lamb with Redcurrant and Wine Sauce

Easy entertaining

Redcurrant jelly is a marvellous ingredient for adding to savoury sauces and it makes a great red wine sauce for lamb dishes.

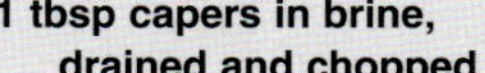

Ingredients for 2

1 tbsp olive oil
2 lamb shanks on the bone,
    each weighing about
    350g/12oz
2 medium onions, quartered
1 small clove garlic, peeled
    and crushed
75g/3oz carrots, sliced
50g/2oz turnips, peeled
    and cubed
75ml/2½fl oz lamb or beef
    stock
1 tbsp tomato purée
75ml/2½fl oz red wine
1½ tbsp redcurrant jelly
1 tsp Worcestershire sauce
1 sprig of fresh rosemary
1 tsp capers in brine,
    drained and chopped

Ingredients for 4

2 tbsp olive oil
4 lamb shanks on the bone,
    each weighing about
    350g/12oz
4 medium onions, quartered
1 clove garlic, peeled
    and crushed
175g/6oz carrots, sliced
100g/4oz turnips, peeled
    and cubed
150ml/¼pt lamb or beef
    stock
2 tbsp tomato purée
150ml/¼pt red wine
3 tbsp redcurrant jelly
1 tbsp Worcestershire sauce
2 sprigs of fresh rosemary
1 tbsp capers in brine,
    drained and chopped

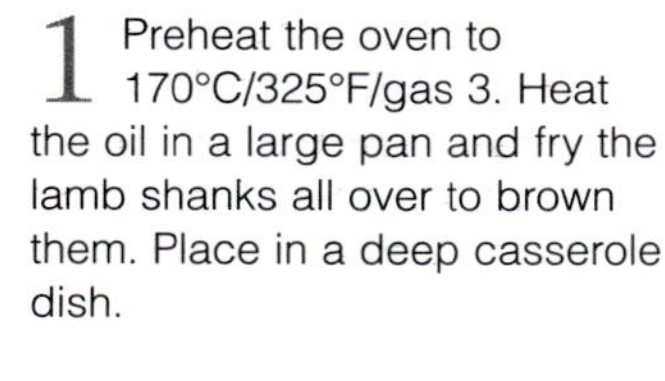

1 Preheat the oven to 170°C/325°F/gas 3. Heat the oil in a large pan and fry the lamb shanks all over to brown them. Place in a deep casserole dish.

2 Add the onions to the pan and fry until browned, then add to the casserole. Add the garlic, carrots and turnips to the pan and fry over a medium heat for 3 minutes. Add the stock, tomato purée, red wine, redcurrant jelly, Worcestershire sauce and rosemary.

3 Pour the liquid into the casserole dish and cover with a lid or a piece of foil. Bake for 2 hours.

4 Add the chopped capers and cook for a further 30 minutes or until the lamb is tender and falls from the bone. Add fresh rosemary to garnish and serve with sautéed potatoes.

Tip

Cool and freeze in polythene freezer bags. They will keep for 3 months. To use, thaw for 8 hours and gently reheat in a pan over a medium heat.

Summer Pudding

Delicious desserts

This traditional combination of black- and redcurrants and raspberries really captures the flavours of summer. If you have a lot of fresh berries to use up, make one or two extra puddings for the freezer.

Ingredients
Serves 8

**9 slices of white bread,
  one day old**
**250g/9oz blackcurrants,
  topped and tailed**
**250g/9 oz redcurrants,
  topped and tailed**
**325g/11oz raspberries,
  hulled**
100g/4oz caster sugar
2 tbsp crème de cassis

1 Line a 1l/1¾pt pudding bowl with cling wrap. Place a piece of bread underneath the bowl as a guide, and cut around it. Place the circle of bread inside the base of the bowl. Cut the crusts from the remaining slices and line the inside of the bowl, overlapping the bread to make sure there are no gaps. Keep the remaining bread to cover the top.

2 Place the currants in a small pan with the sugar and cassis and bring to a simmer for 3 minutes until softened.

3 Add the raspberries and simmer for 2 minutes. Stir well, and spoon the warm fruit into the bowl, with enough juice to soak into the bread. Keep back any remaining juice.

4 Cut the remaining bread to fit over the top of the bowl and tuck in neatly. Cover with cling wrap and a plate and a can to weigh down the pudding, then chill overnight. To serve, unwrap the top and place a plate over the pudding. Upturn the bowl, lift away the bowl and pour over any remaining juice. Serve with thick cream.

Tip

To freeze, place the pudding in the basin and wrap in foil. It will keep for 6 months once frozen. To use, thaw for 12 hours then remove the pudding basin and serve.

Redcurrant Jelly

Store-cupboard special

Sharp and tangy, redcurrant jelly is traditionally served with roast lamb or lamb cutlets, but it is also delicious served with poultry or game. It is an indispensable ingredient to have in your store cupboard as it makes a superb glaze for red fruit tarts or pastries or a delicious addition to red wine sauces and braised meat dishes.

Ingredients
Makes 1.5kg/3lb jelly

1.5kg/3lb redcurrants, washed

600ml/1pt water
Granulated sugar (see method)

1 Leaving the redcurrants on their stalks, place them in a large pan with the water and simmer very gently until the fruit is soft.

2 Pour the fruit and juice from the pan into a muslin jelly bag or a doubled square of muslin suspended over a large bowl. Leave the pulp to drip slowly through the muslin into the bowl for eight hours or overnight.

3 Measure the red juice extract that has dripped into the bowl in a jug. Weigh out 450g/1lb sugar for each 600ml/1pt of red juice extract measured. Place the extract and the sugar in a large heavy-based pan and simmer over a low heat until every grain of sugar has dissolved.

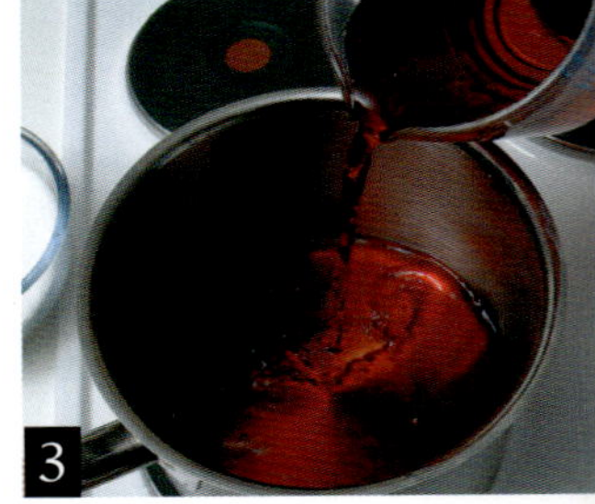

4 Boil until setting point has been reached (see plate test, page 22). Pour into small, warmed, sterilised jars (see page 23) and cover with waxed discs, wax side down, then cool, cover and label. The jelly will set rapidly so work very quickly.

Tip
Store in a cool, dark place for up to a year. Once opened, store the jar in the refrigerator, or mould may develop on the surface.

Blackcurrant Cheesecake

Freezer friendly

This delicate cheesecake makes a delicious dessert and is ideal to make and store in the freezer.

Ingredients
Makes a 20cm/8in cheescake

75g/3oz butter, melted
1 tbsp golden syrup
225g/8oz digestive biscuits, crushed
225g/8oz blackcurrants, topped and tailed
15g/½oz sachet gelatine
175g/6oz crème fraîche

200g/7oz cream cheese, softened
75g/3oz icing sugar
1 tbsp lemon juice
150ml/¼pt natural yoghurt
Whites from 2 medium eggs
140ml/¼pt whipping cream, whipped, to decorate
Blackcurrant sprigs on stalks, to decorate

1 Grease and line the base and sides of a 20cm/8in spring-clipped cake tin with non-stick baking paper. To make the biscuit base, melt the butter and syrup together in a small pan and stir in the crushed biscuit crumbs. Press the warm mixture over the base of the tin, and chill while making the filling.

2 Place the blackcurrants in a processor or liquidiser and blend to a purée. Sprinkle the gelatine over 3 tbsp cold water and heat gently in a small bowl in a pan of hot water, or in the microwave oven on a medium setting, until melted.

3 Stir the cream cheese with the crème fraîche, icing sugar, lemon juice and yoghurt. Stir in the gelatine and blackcurrant purée. Whisk the egg whites until stiff, then gently fold into the mixture.

4 Pour into the tin over the biscuit base and leave to chill until set, about 1 hour. To serve, release from the tin, peel away the lining paper and decorate the top with piped cream and blackcurrants.

Tip

To freeze, leave undecorated in the tin and wrap with foil. It will keep for 6 months. To use, thaw in the tin for 8 hours, remove the sides of the tin and decorate as above.

Blackcurrant Jam

Perfect preserves

In the winter months you will appreciate this delightful jam, as it is packed full of vitamin C, and its tart flavour will be a welcome taste of summer on cold mornings. Make picking blackcurrants an easy job by snipping whole stalks of fruit away from the branches with scissors.

Ingredients
Makes 3kg/7lb

1.5kg/3lb blackcurrants
1.2l/2pt water

1.8kg/4lb golden granulated or preserving sugar

1 Strip the blackcurrants away from the stalks using the tines of a fork and trim away any brown ends or leaves. Wash and drain well then place in a large pan or preserving pan with the water.

2 Simmer gently until the fruit is softened and the mixture has reduced. As the skin on blackcurrants tends to be tough, cook the mixture well and stir often to prevent the base of the pan from burning.

3 When the fruit is soft, add the sugar and stir over a low heat until every grain has dissolved. Bring up the heat and boil rapidly until setting point has been reached (see plate test, page 22).

4 Pour into warmed, sterilised jars (see page 23) and cover with waxed discs, wax side down while still hot. Leave until cold then cover and label with name and date.

Tip

If you are using your own frozen blackcurrants, it is easy to remove any stalks from these while still frozen. Simply rub the hard berries and the stalks will brush away.

Grated Blackberry Bake

Family favourite

If you are lucky enough to have a blackberry hedge nearby, make the most of their harvest in the autumn months. Once the berries start to ripen they will be in abundance for about a month and are ideal for freezing or baking into pastries and puddings.

Ingredients
Makes a 21cm/81/2in cake

350g/12oz blackberries
175g/6oz granulated sugar
275g/10oz plain flour
A pinch of salt

**Finely grated zest of ½
    lemon**
**175g/6oz butter or block
    margarine**
100g/4oz golden caster sugar
1 medium egg, beaten

1 Remove any leaves and stalks, lightly rinse the blackberries and drain well. Place the fruit in a pan with 2 tablespoons of water and simmer for 8 minutes until softened. Stir in the sugar and raise the heat until boiling. Cook for 4-5 minutes, stirring regularly, until thick. Leave to cool while you make the pastry.

2 Sift the flour and salt into a bowl and stir in the lemon zest. Cut the fat into pieces, then rub or process them until the mixture resembles fine crumbs. Stir in the sugar and beaten egg and mix together to form a dough. Wrap in a plastic bag and chill for 1 hour or freeze for 10 minutes to firm the dough.

3 Preheat the oven to 200°C/400°F/gas 6. Grease the sides and base of a round 21cm (8½in) spring-clipped cake tin and line the base with a disc of non-stick baking paper.

4 Cut the chilled pastry in half. Coarsely grate one half of the pastry over the base of the tin and press down lightly. Spread the cooled filling over the top. Grate the other half of the pastry over the filling, taking it right to the edges to prevent the filling bubbling up. Bake for 35-40 minutes until the topping is golden. Cool for 5 minutes, then remove the sides of the tin and cut the bake into wedges. Serve hot with custard or cream, or cold as a cake, dusted with icing sugar.

Blackberry Meringue Roulade

Easy entertaining

This special dessert has a delicate sponge base that is as light as a feather, filled with fresh cream and juicy blackberries.

Ingredients
Serves 6/8

450g/1lb blackberries
50g/2oz icing sugar
3 medium eggs

75g/3oz caster sugar
50g/2oz plain flour
450ml/¾pt whipping cream
100g/4oz blackberries
Sprigs of fresh mint

1 Preheat the oven to 180°C/350°F/gas mark 4. Line a 23x33cm/9x13in Swiss roll tin with non-stick baking paper and brush lightly with oil.

2 Place the blackberries in a processor or liquidiser and blend to a purée with 25g/1oz icing sugar. Pour through a fine sieve and discard the pips.

3 Whisk the eggs and caster sugar together in a bowl standing over a pan of hot water, until the mixture has doubled in volume and is thick. Fold the flour and the blackberry purée into the egg mixture and pour into the prepared tin. Spread into the corners evenly, and bake for about 20 minutes. Cool on a wire rack and cover the top with a cloth or damp kitchen paper while hot to help rolling.

4 Sprinkle the remaining icing sugar over a sheet of greaseproof paper. Turn the roulade out onto the paper, peel away the lining paper and trim away the outer edges. Whip the cream until thick and spread two thirds over the roulade. Sprinkle with half the blackberries and roll up using the greaseproof paper. Place the remaining cream in a piping bag and pipe rosettes on top of the roll. Place a blackberry and a sprig of mint in each one.

Tip

Freeze the roulade, rolled up with cream in, but undecorated and wrapped in foil. It will keep for 3 months. To use, thaw for 1-2 hours at room temperature, then decorate as above.

Blackberry and Apple Turnover

Family favourite

This flaky golden pastry is packed with tasty fruit and it makes an ideal dessert for a family lunch or supper.

Ingredients
Makes 4

275g/10oz Bramley cooking apples
Finely grated zest of ½ lemon
15g/½ oz butter
40g/1½oz golden caster sugar
225g/8oz blackberries
250g/9oz ready-made puff pastry
1 medium egg
2 tbsp golden caster sugar

1 Peel and core the apples, then cut into thick slices. Put the slices in a pan with the lemon zest, sugar, butter and 2 tbsp cold water. Simmer, covered, for 5 minutes or until the apples are still firm but tender and the water has evaporated. Turn off the heat add the blackberries and leave to cool.

2 Preheat the oven to 200°C/400°F/gas mark 6. Grease a baking sheet and roll out the pastry to a 30cm/12in square.

3 Place the pastry on the baking sheet, leaving the edges overlapping the tray. Spoon the cooled filling into the centre. Brush the pastry edges lightly with water and bring the four corners into the centre, like an envelope. Seal the edges together, making a fluted edge and a neat square parcel.

4 Beat the egg with 1 tbsp cold water and brush over the top. Sprinkle over the sugar and bake for 20-25 minutes until the pastry has puffed up and is light golden. Cut into wedges and serve hot with thick cream or custard.

Tip
Not suitable for freezing.

Giant Blueberry Cookies

Quick and easy

Blueberries are packed with good things and have a lovely jammy flavour when they are heated, as they pop open.

Ingredients
Makes 12

75g/3oz butter or block margarine, softened
175g/6oz soft, light brown sugar

Finely grated zest of 1 lemon
½ tsp vanilla essence
1 medium egg
175g/6oz self-raising flour
100g/4oz fresh blueberries

1 Preheat the oven to 180°C/350°F/gas mark 4. Grease two baking sheets.

2 Place the butter, sugar and lemon zest in a large bowl and beat together until the mixture is light and fluffy. Beat the vanilla essence with the egg and gradually add to the mixture with a tablespoon of flour to prevent the mixture from separating.

3 Sift the flour into the bowl and mix with your fingertips to make a soft but firm dough. Divide into 12 pieces and place on the greased baking sheets.

4 Roughly shape each mound of dough into a round shape. Divide the blueberries between the rounds and press them into each cookie. Bake for 12-14 minutes until light and golden. Leave to cool on the baking sheets for 5 minutes to allow the biscuit to become firm, then remove to cool on a wire rack. Best eaten on the day of baking.

Tip

Cool and freeze the cookies shortly after baking. Pack in freezer boxes. They will keep for 2 months. To use, thaw on wire racks for 2-3 hours, and eat immediately.

Blueberry and Cinnamon Muffins

Family favourite

Freshly baked, homemade muffins are always popular for breakfast or tea. These are packed with bursting juicy berries and are delicious served warm, soon after baking.

Ingredients
Serves 6/8

50g/2oz butter, melted
225g/8oz plain flour
1 tbsp baking powder
½ tsp bicarbonate of soda
1 tsp ground cinnamon

10g/4oz caster sugar
1 medium egg
250ml/8floz milk
A pinch of salt
100g/4oz fresh blueberries
Deep, paper muffin cases

1 Preheat the oven to 200°C/400°F/gas mark 6. Place nine deep, paper muffin cases in a deep muffin tray. Melt the butter in a small pan and leave to cool slightly for 5 minutes.

2 Sift all the dry ingredients together into a bowl, stir in the sugar and make a well in the centre. Beat the egg, milk and salt together.

3 Stir the milk mixture into the bowl with the melted butter. Lightly beat, leaving the mixture slightly lumpy. Do not over-beat the mixture it should not be smooth. Fold in the blueberries.

4 Fill each muffin case three-quarters full, and bake for about 20 minutes or until a skewer inserted into the centre of each muffin comes out cleanly. Serve warm or cold. Eat or freeze the muffins within 24 hours.

Tip

To freeze, bake and cool the muffins and pack in rigid polythene boxes. They will keep for 3 months. To use, thaw at room temperature for 2 hours.

Sweet Cherry Clafouti

Delicious desserts

Dark, sweet morello cherries are delicious but have a very short season. If you are lucky enough to have a cherry tree in your garden you will look forward every year to picking this sweetest of fruits. This hot dessert is based on a sweet batter and comes from the south of France, where cherries are plentiful.

Ingredients
Serves 4

700g/1½lb dark cherries, pitted
4 tbsp orange liqueur, such as Cointreau, or orange juice
125ml/4fl oz milk
150ml/¼pt double cream

Finely grated zest of 1 orange
4 medium eggs
100g/4oz caster sugar
25g/1oz plain flour
Icing sugar for dusting
300ml/½pt single cream, to serve

1 Butter a shallow 800ml/ 1½pt (1.7l/3pt) ovenproof dish. Heat the cherries gently in the liqueur or orange juice and set aside to cool for 15 minutes. Heat the oven to 180°C/350°F/gas mark 4.

2 Bring the milk, cream and orange zest to the boil in a small pan. Remove from the heat and allow to infuse for 15 minutes.

3 Strain the cherries and reserve the soaking liquid.

Place the cherries in the base of the buttered dish. Whisk the eggs and sugar until thick. Gradually add the flour and whisk until smooth.

4 Whisk in the cream mixture and 1 tsp (1 tbsp) of the reserved cooking liquor. Pour over the cherries in the dish and bake for 50 minutes to 1 hour, until firm and golden. Dust with icing sugar. Stir the remaining liquor into the single cream to flavour it and serve with the hot pudding.

Tip

Not suitable for freezing.

Black Forest Chocolate Roulade

something special

Make the base for this dessert the evening before it is needed. It will become moist overnight and all you need to do is to fill it with cream and plump fresh cherries just before you serve it.

Ingredients
Serves 6/8

2 tsp instant coffee granules
100g/4oz plain chocolate,
melted

4 medium eggs, separated
100g/4oz golden caster sugar
300ml/½ pt whipping cream
450g/1lb ripe fresh cherries
Icing sugar for dusting

1 Preheat the oven to 180°C/350°F/gas mark 4. Grease and line a 28x33cm/11x13in Swiss roll tin with non-stick baking paper. Blend the coffee to a smooth paste with 1 tbsp warm water.

2 Whisk the egg yolks and sugar together in a bowl over a pan of hot water until thick and pale. Remove from the heat and stir in the cooled melted chocolate and coffee mixture. Whisk the egg whites until stiff then fold 3 tbsp into the chocolate mixture to loosen it. Fold in the remaining egg whites carefully.

3 Spread the mixture into the tin and bake for about 15 minutes, until the top is firm. Cover with a clean, damp cloth and leave for 8 hours or overnight if possible. Sprinkle a large sheet of greaseproof paper with icing sugar and turn the cake out onto it.

4 Peel away the lining paper and trim away the crusty edges of the roll. Whip the cream and spread two thirds over the roulade. Remove the stones from three-quarters of the cherries and keep the rest for decoration. Scatter the pitted cherries over the sponge and roll up the cake using the paper to guide it. Dust with icing sugar and pipe the remaining cream on top. Decorate with the remaining cherries.

Tip
Not suitable for freezing.

Zucotto Cream Dessert

Freezer friendly

The sweet-and-sour flavour of rich dark cherries makes a perfect partner to this creamy white chocolate dessert. Once you have tried the cherry sauce, you will find it becomes a family favourite to serve with ice creams or pancakes.

Ingredients
Serves 8

150g/5oz white chocolate
250g/9oz tub of mascarpone soft cheese
150ml/¼pt double cream
225g/8oz dark chocolate biscuits, crushed
50g/2oz butter

Cherry sauce

1 tbsp arrowroot
100ml/3½fl oz cold water
150ml/¼pt crème de cassis
450g/1lb cherries, stalks removed

1 Brush the inside of a 450g/1lb loaf tin with oil then line with cling wrap, smoothing out any creases. Break the white chocolate into pieces and melt gently in a bowl over a pan of simmering water or in the microwave on a low setting, stirring frequently.

2 Place the mascarpone in a bowl and stir to soften. Whip the cream until it forms soft peaks then fold into the mascarpone. Add the melted chocolate and fold together. Pour into the tin and smooth the top level.

3 Crush the biscuits to crumbs in a strong plastic bag or in a food processor. Melt the butter and mix into the crushed biscuit crumbs. Sprinkle over the top of the cream mixture in the tin and smooth level. Chill for 1 hour or until firm.

4 To make the sauce, mix the arrowroot to a paste with 1 tbsp water taken from the cold water. Place in a pan with the remaining water, and the crème de cassis. Bring to the boil and stir until clear and thick. Add the cherries and heat for 3 minutes. Cool for 5 minutes before serving.

5 To serve, invert the solid mousse onto a plate and cut into slices. Serve each slice with a spoonful of cherries and sauce.

Damson Gin

Damson gin is a delicious, mellow liqueur that you can easily make at home. If you use damsons picked in late summer, it will be ready for drinking over Christmas, when you can welcome your guests in from the cold with a delicious warming glass.

Ingredients
Makes 2 x 425ml (14fl oz) bottles

450g/1lb damsons, washed
175g/6oz granulated sugar
700ml/1¼pt gin

1 Drain and dry the damsons thoroughly. Prick each damson all over with a fork or a small skewer.

2 Half fill a clean glass jar with the fruit and pour in the sugar. Use a funnel if the jar has a narrow neck.

3 Leave the sugar and fruit in the jar for several hours to allow the juices to run from the fruit.

4 Pour in enough gin to bring the level up to the top of the jar or bottle, covering the fruit. Seal the jar with a lid and store in a cool place, away from direct sunlight. Each day, tip the jar upside down and shake to dissolve the sugar and release the damson juices.

5 Once the sugar has dissolved, leave the gin to stand for three months. Strain the gin into sterile bottles, leaving a few damsons in the base of each bottle for decoration.

Variation
Sloe gin can be made in the same way. Pick wild sloes from the hedgerows, wash and drain them. As sloes are much smaller than damsons, prick them with a large pin or a small skewer. Follow the recipe above, leaving the sloes to macerate in the sugar, then adding the gin.

Damson Cobbler

You cannot eat damsons raw, because they have such a sharp flavour, but add some sugar and a fluffy cobbler topping and you have a real old-fashioned family pudding that you cannot resist.

Ingredients for 2

1 Bramley cooking apple
225g/8oz damsons, washed
    and trimmed
40g/1½oz caster sugar
100g/4oz self-raising flour
A pinch ground cinnamon
25g/1oz butter
40g/1½oz caster sugar
45ml/1½fl oz milk, plus
    extra for glazing

Ingredients for 4

2 Bramley cooking apples
450g/1lb damsons, washed
    and trimmed
75g/3oz caster sugar
225g/8oz self-raising flour
½ tsp ground cinnamon
50g/2oz butter
75g/3oz caster sugar
90ml/3fl oz milk, plus extra
    for glazing

1 Peel and core the apples and cut into large chunks. Place the apples in a pan with the damsons and sugar. Cover and simmer for 10 minutes until the apples begin to soften, but do not break up. Place the fruit in a buttered 800ml/1½pt (1.7l/3pt) ovenproof dish.

2 Preheat the oven to 220°C/425°F/gas mark 7. Make the topping. Sift the flour and cinnamon into a bowl or processor. Cut the butter into small cubes and add to the bowl. Rub the fat into the flour or process until the mixture resembles fine crumbs. Stir in the sugar and add enough milk to make a soft dough.

3 Roll out on a lightly floured surface to 1cm/½in thickness. Cut into rounds or fancy shapes with a pastry cutter.

4 Arrange the pastry shapes on top of the fruit in the dish in a jumble, overlapping some of them. Brush with milk and bake for 15-20 minutes until the topping is golden and puffy. Serve hot with custard or thick cream.

Tip

Remind your guests that the stones remain in the damsons!

Warm Fig and Proscuitto Salad

Easy entertaining

If you are lucky enough to have a fig tree with abundant fruit in the autumn, try serving them as a first course. Fresh figs are delicious served as a starter with a Mediterranean-style salad. Gently warming the figs releases their flavour and sweetness.

Ingredients for 2

2 tbsp olive oil
½ tbsp clear honey
½ tbsp balsamic vinegar
½ tbsp cranberry sauce
1 small orange
2 ripe figs
50g/2oz mozzarella cheese, sliced
4 slices wafer-thin prosciutto ham
Basil and fresh rocket to garnish

Ingredients for 4

4 tbsp olive oil
1 tbsp clear honey
1 tbsp balsamic vinegar
1 tbsp cranberry sauce
1 orange
4 ripe figs
100g/4oz mozzarella cheese, sliced
8 slices wafer-thin prosciutto ham
Basil and fresh rocket to garnish

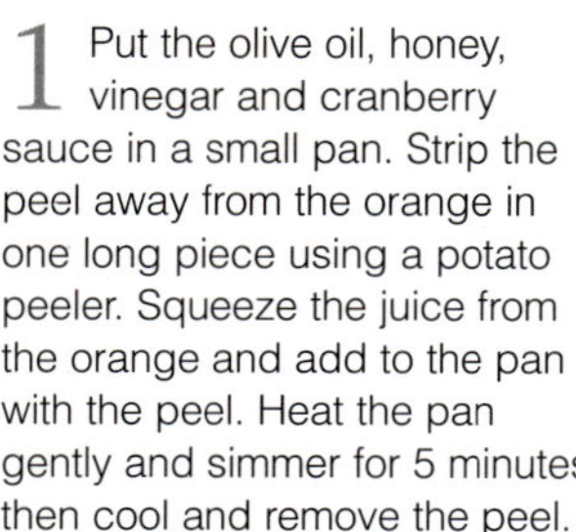

1 Put the olive oil, honey, vinegar and cranberry sauce in a small pan. Strip the peel away from the orange in one long piece using a potato peeler. Squeeze the juice from the orange and add to the pan with the peel. Heat the pan gently and simmer for 5 minutes, then cool and remove the peel.

2 Preheat a grill to hot. Cut a cross in the top of each fig and gently squeeze to open out the fruit, leaving the base intact.

Lightly brush a little of the dressing over each fig and place on the grill. Grill for 1-2 minutes until warmed through but not brown.

3 Arrange slices of mozzarella and ham on each plate with basil and rocket leaves.

4 Add a warm fig to each plate and drizzle over the remaining dressing. Serve immediately.

Tip

Not suitable for freezing.

Figs in Brandy

Store-cupboard special

When figs are plentiful, make this preserve for your winter store cupboard. These alcohol-infused fruits are wonderful served after dinner with coffee and petits fours or with creamy desserts such as panna cotta

Ingredients

Makes two large jars of 8 figs or 4 small jars of 4 figs

1kg/2lb ripe, firm-fleshed figs
(about 16 figs)
16 walnut halves
1 lemon
450g/1lb granulated sugar
8-10 tbsp of brandy

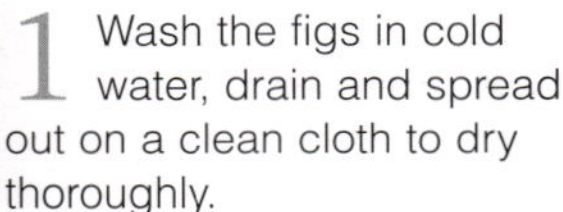

1 Wash the figs in cold water, drain and spread out on a clean cloth to dry thoroughly.

2 Cut down each fig lengthways, leaving the two halves attached. Press a walnut half into the centre of each fig and close the two halves together.

3 Peel the zest from the lemon in long, thin strips and squeeze out the juice. Pack the figs in layers into clean, dry preserving jars, sprinkling between each layer with sugar. Place a piece of lemon zest and 2 tsp of lemon juice in each jar.

4 Spoon 2-3 tbsp brandy into each jar. When the jar is filled to within 1cm/½in of its neck, fill to the top with a few tablespoons of boiling water. Seal the jars by clamping down the wire-clipped tops.

5 Line the base of a large saucepan with a folded sheet of newspaper. Place the jars in the pan and place a folded sheet of newspaper in between them to prevent the jars rattling against each other. Cover with cold water up to their necks. Bring to the boil then simmer for 45 minutes. Allow the jars to cool completely in the water, then lift out and store in a dry, dark place.

Crumbly Gooseberry and Almond Torte

For the cake tin

Gooseberries need not just be made into puddings, jams and desserts. Try this moist almond-based cake with a crunchy topping that goes so well with tart green gooseberries.

Ingredients
Makes a 23cm/9in torte

200g/7oz butter
175g/6oz golden caster sugar
Finely grated zest of 1 lemon
2 medium eggs
½ tsp almond essence

100g/4oz ground almonds
100g/4oz self-raising flour
½ tsp baking powder
225g/8oz green gooseberries, trimmed
25g/1oz Demerara sugar
50g/2oz flaked almonds

1 Preheat the oven to 180°C/350°F/gas mark 4. Grease and line a 23cm/9in round cake tin with baking parchment.

2 Put 175g/6oz butter in a bowl and beat to soften. Add the caster sugar and half the lemon zest and whisk until light and fluffy. Whisk in the eggs and almond essence, adding a spoonful of ground almonds with each addition.

3 Sift the flour and baking powder into the mixture, then fold in the remaining ground almonds. Spoon into the tin and spread level. Bake

for 20 minutes, then open the oven door and sprinkle the gooseberries evenly over the top of the cake. Bake for a further 10 minutes.

4 Melt the remaining 25g/1oz butter and stir in the Demerara sugar, flaked almonds and remaining lemon zest. Open the oven door again and scatter the mixture over the top of the cake. Bake for a further 15 minutes or until a skewer inserted into the centre comes out cleanly. Cool in the tin for 5 minutes and serve warm with thick yoghurt or cream, or cold, sliced as a cake.

Tip

To freeze, cool the cake on a wire rack and freeze wrapped in foil. It will keep for 3 months. To use, thaw at room temperature for 4-6 hours and slice.

Pink Gooseberry Fool

Delicious desserts

If you have gooseberry plants that produce soft pink fruits then use them to make this delicate dessert. It can also be made using green gooseberries, but the pretty pink swirls really are attractive.

Ingredients for 2

225g/8oz pink or green gooseberries, trimmed and washed
50g/2oz caster sugar
1 strip pared lemon peel
1 tbsp elderflower cordial or orange juice
1 tsp custard powder
75ml/2½fl oz milk
75ml/2½fl oz double cream
Sponge finger biscuits, to serve

Ingredients for 4

450g/1lb pink or green gooseberries, trimmed and washed
100g/4oz caster sugar
2 strips pared lemon peel
2 tbsp elderflower cordial or orange juice
1 tbsp custard powder
150ml/¼pt milk
150ml/¼pt double cream
Sponge finger biscuits, to serve

1 Place the fruit, sugar and peels in a heavy-based pan and cook over a low heat for about 10 minutes, until the fruit is soft. Remove the lemon peel.

2 Place the softened fruit in a liquidiser or processor and blend to a purée with the elderflower cordial or orange juice.

3 Blend the custard powder with 1 tbsp (2 tbsp) of the milk to a smooth paste in a bowl. Heat the remaining milk to just below boiling then pour over the paste and stir well. Return to the pan and heat until thickened, stirring frequently.

4 Pour the custard into a bowl, stir in the gooseberry purée and leave to cool. Whip the cream until it forms soft peaks, and swirl into the puréed mixture. Serve in glass dishes, with sponge finger biscuits.

Tip

Not suitable for freezing.

Pink Gooseberry Jam

Perfect preserves

The varieties of gooseberries that bear fruit with a pink blush are perfect for making this delicious jam, which has a delicate pink hue. You can also use the green varieties, which will produce a light green jam.

Ingredients
Makes 900g/2lb

700g/1½lb pink
   gooseberries

150ml/¼pt water
700g/1½lb granulated or
   jam sugar
A knob of butter

1 Trim the tops and tails from the gooseberries with kitchen scissors, wash the fruit and drain. Place the fruit in a heavy-based pan with the water and simmer for about 12 minutes, until the fruit is softened.

2 Stir in the sugar and cook over a low heat for 3-4 minutes, stirring, until every grain of sugar has dissolved.

3 Turn up the heat and cook, uncovered for about 15 minutes then start to test for setting point (see plate test, page 22).

4 Test for a set every minute to prevent overcooking and when the jam has reached setting point add the butter, stir, and pour into warmed sterilised jars (see page 23). Cover with waxed discs, wax side down, cover with tops and label when cool.

Tip 1

To make in a microwave oven, place the fruit and water in a large microwave-proof bowl and cook on a high setting for 8-10 minutes, until the fruit is soft. Stir in the sugar and cook uncovered for 2 minutes on a high setting until the sugar dissolves. Continue to cook, uncovered, on a high setting for 15-20 minutes until setting point is reached.

Tip 2

This recipe makes a smaller amount of jam than usual. If you want to make more, simply double the quantities and simmer in a large, heavy-based preserving pan.

Rumpot

Store-cupboard special

These layers of fresh summer fruits are soaked in a rich rum syrup. Start the rumpot with strawberries, then cherries and add fruits as they come into season. Loganberries and tayberries are a particularly good addition as they add a dark contrast to the lighter fruits and have a wonderful tangy rich flavour

Ingredients

225g/8oz caster sugar for every 450g/1lb of prepared fruits
Enough dark rum to cover the fruit

Use: loganberries, tayberries, strawberries, cherries, apricots, raspberries, plums, redcurrants, peaches, grapes.

1 Wash a large wide-necked jar in hot soapy water, rinse and leave upside down to drain dry. Wash the fruits, drain and dry well on kitchen paper to remove all moisture. Remove all stalks, hulls and stones.

2 Spread the dry fruit out on a plate and coat it in the caster sugar. Leave the fruit to stand for 1 hour then place in the jar in one layer.

3 Pour in enough rum to cover the layer. Put a small, clean plate over the fruit to keep it submerged in the syrup. Wrap the top of the jar with cling wrap and replace the lid. Store in a cool dark place until you are ready to add the next layer of fruit.

4 Repeat with a different layer of sugar-coated fruit, top up with rum, cover with the plate and reseal. When the last layer has been added, top up with more rum, seal tightly and store in a cool dark place for 13 months to allow the flavours of the fruits and the rum to blend together.

Tip

Avoid citrus fruit, apples, bananas, pears and rhubarb which give off sour flavours. Also avoid melons, as they are watery and will dilute the syrup and cause mould. The fruits must be sound, whole and ripe and it is possible to use just a few fruits at a time as they come into season. Use a large preserving jar or a stone crock to layer the fruits, with a wide neck that will take 5-8l/9-14pt capacity. Store the crock in a cool dark place.

Peach Conserve

This delicate preserve has a light set, as it contains less sugar than usual, so store it in the refrigerator after opening. This recipe makes a smaller amount of jam, which needs less boiling and keeps the delicate flavours of the peaches.

Ingredients
Makes 1.9kg/4lb

1kg/2¼lb peaches
½ lemon
225ml/8fl oz water

700g/1½lb sugar
A knob of butter
125ml/4fl oz commercial pectin

1 Skin, stone and chop the peaches, reserving the stones. Squeeze the juice from the lemon. Chop the halved lemon peel and tie up in a square of muslin with the peach stones.

2 Put the chopped peaches, lemon juice, water and the muslin bag in a deep heavy-based pan and simmer for 20-30 minutes, until the peaches are tender.

3 Remove the muslin bag and squeeze it. Add the sugar and stir until completely dissolved. Add the butter and bring to the boil, then boil for 5-10 minutes.

4 Remove from the heat and stir in the pectin. Boil for a minute only. Remove any scum and allow the jam to cool slightly. Pour into warmed, sterilised jars (see page 23), then cover with waxed discs, wax side down. Cover and label when cold.

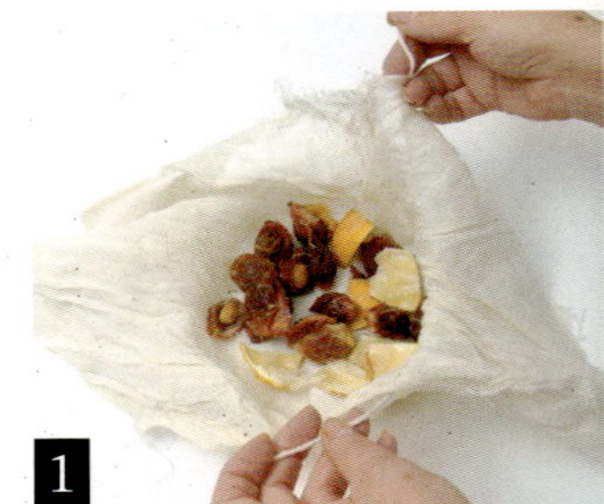

Tip

As this recipe contains less sugar, and peaches are a fruit low in pectin, liquid pectin is added to make it set. This can be bought in small bottles in supermarkets or chemists' stores.

Peaches in Brandy

If you are fortunate enough to have a glut of peaches, you will find preserving them in brandy is a worthwhile exercise. Keep them in the store cupboard and enjoy their delicate flavour in the winter months, along with the delicious brandy syrup.

Ingredients
Makes 1.5kg/3lb

1.5kg/3lb firm peaches
1 l/1¾pt water
1.5kg/3lb granulated sugar

1 vanilla pod
1 cinnamon stick
4 whole cloves
300ml/½pt brandy

1 Blanch the peaches in boiling water for a few seconds then dip them into cold water and slip the skins away. Halve the peaches and cut away the stones.

2 Put the water and 450g/1lb sugar into a heavy-based pan. Heat to dissolve then bring to the boil and simmer for 5 minutes to make a syrup.

3 Lift the peaches into the syrup with a slotted spoon. Bring to the boil and simmer for 5 minutes. Lift the peaches out of the syrup with a slotted spoon, drain and cool. Tie the spices in a piece of muslin to make a small bag. Place 600ml/1pt of the syrup in a pan with the remaining sugar and the muslin spice bag.

4 Heat gently to dissolve the sugar grains then bring to the boil and boil rapidly for 5 minutes until thick, syrupy and reduced. Cool for 10 minutes, then remove the bag of spices and stir in the brandy. Pack the peaches into warmed sterilised jars (see page 23) and pour the syrup over them to cover completely. Shake to remove any pockets of air, cover and seal. Keep the peaches for 2 weeks before use. Store in a cool, dark place out or sunlight They will keep for 2-3 years.

Baked Stuffed Peaches

Delicious dessert

This quick-and-easy dessert is ideal to serve after a barbecue. Prepare the dish of peaches ahead of time and bake it for just 30 minutes when you need it.

Ingredients for 2

3 ripe peaches
25g/1oz amaretti biscuits
½ tsp lemon juice
25g/1oz vanilla caster sugar
15g/½ oz flaked almonds
2 tbsp dessert wine or
    sweet sherry

Ingredients for 4

6 ripe peaches
50g/2oz amaretti biscuits
1 tsp lemon juice
50g/2oz vanilla caster sugar
25g/1oz flaked almonds
4 tbsp dessert wine or
    sweet sherry

1 Preheat the oven to 180°C/350°F/gas mark 4. Cut two (four) peaches in half and remove the stones. Butter a shallow ovenproof dish and then place 4 (8) peach halves in the base, cut side up.

2 Skin and stone the one (two) remaining peach(es) and mash the flesh with a fork to a rough purée. Crush the amaretti biscuits and stir into the peach purée with the lemon juice and half the sugar.

3 Press the mixture into the hollow peach halves and scatter over the almonds and remaining sugar.

4 Spoon the wine round the fruit and bake for 30 minutes or until golden. Serve warm with thick cream or yoghurt.

Tip

If you do not want to use wine or sherry, use fresh orange juice instead.

Frangipane and Chocolate Pear Tart

Something special

Sweet juicy pears and chocolate make an irresistible combination. Make this tart ahead of time for a tea or supper party, or keep a few slices in the freezer for a treat.

Ingredients
Makes a 23cm/9in tart

250g/9oz ready-made shortcrust pastry
100g/4oz plain chocolate, broken into pieces
50g/2oz butter
100g/4oz ground almonds
2 large pears, peeled, halved and cored
2 medium eggs, separated
50g/2oz caster sugar

1 Preheat the oven to 180°C/350°F/gas mark 4. Grease a 23cm/9in fluted loose-based deep tart tin. Roll out the pastry on a lightly floured surface and use to line the tin. Trim the edges neatly, then chill in the freezer while preparing the filling.

2 Place the chocolate pieces in a bowl standing over a pan of simmering water. When melted, remove from the heat, add the butter and stir until smooth. Stir in the ground almonds and leave to cool.

3 Slice the pear halves thinly, keeping each pear half together. Whisk the egg yolks and sugar until thick and pale and fold into the cooled chocolate mixture.

4 Whisk the egg whites until stiff and fold into the chocolate mixture. Spoon the mixture into the pastry case. Press the sliced pear halves into the chocolate mixture. Bake for 50 minutes to 1 hour, until the centre is firm. If the top starts to burn, cover with foil. Serve hot or cold dusted with icing sugar.

Tip

To freeze, bake the tart, cool and wrap in foil. It will keep for 2 months. To use, thaw at room temperature for 2-3 hours before serving.

Pink Pears Poached in Rosé Wine

Easy entertaining

Make this simple and elegant dessert ahead of time and leave it to chill until needed.

Ingredients for 2

150ml/¼pt rosé wine
1 tbsp lemon juice
One long strip of lemon peel
50g/2oz caster sugar
1 vanilla pod
150ml/¼pt water
2 firm pears, peeled and
   halved

Ingredients for 4

300ml/½pt rosé wine
2 tbsp lemon juice
One long strip of lemon peel
100g/4oz caster sugar
1 vanilla pod
300ml/½pt water
4 firm pears, peeled and
   halved

1 Place the wine, lemon juice, peel, caster sugar and vanilla pod in a large heavy-based saucepan with the water. Heat gently to dissolve every grain of sugar.

2 Add the pear halves to the wine mixture and bring to the boil. Turn down the heat and simmer, covered, for about 12 minutes until the pears look slightly translucent.

3 Lift the pears out of the liquid and place them in a bowl. Heat the cooking liquid and boil for 5-8 minutes to reduce it to a thick syrup.

4 Take the syrup off the heat and cool for 5 minutes. Strain over the pears and leave them to cool and chill in the syrup. Chill in the refrigerator for at least 1 hour before serving. Serve two pear halves per person with syrup. Serve with thick Greek yoghurt or crème fraîche.

Tip

Not suitable for freezing.

Open Plum Tart

You can create this juicy plum tart with its delicious flaky pastry base in less than an hour.

Ingredients

Makes a 30x25cm/ 12x10in tart

375g/13oz pack ready-made puff pastry

1 medium egg, beaten
8 large plums, about 700g /1½lb weight
2 tbsp caster sugar

1 Preheat the oven to 200°C/400°F/gas mark 6 and sprinkle a baking sheet lightly with water. Roll the pastry out to a rectangle 30x25cm/12x10in and place on the baking sheet.

2 With a sharp knife, mark a border 1cm/½in in from the edge, but do not cut right through the pastry. Prick the centre all over with the tines of a fork. Brush the border edges with beaten egg.

3 Halve the plums, then cut into quarters, removing the stones. Arrange the plums, cut sides up, over the pastry centre, up to the border edges.

4 Sprinkle over the caster sugar. Bake for 25-30 minutes until the pastry is golden and puffed up and the plums are tender and have a light brown glaze on top where the sugar has melted and cooked. Serve with thick cream.

Tip

Use red-skinned Victoria plums or golden plums for this recipe. You can also use greengages and apricots instead. Not suitable for freezing.

Plum and Tamarind Salsa

Perfect preserves

This spicy accompaniment is a fresh, uncooked chutney, which needs no long boiling. It has a crunchy texture and is ideal to serve with cold meats such as ham, pork or with cheeses. You can also serve it with vegetarian or Thai curries.

Ingredients
Makes 500g/1lb 2oz

450g/14oz Victoria or dark, firm plums, stoned and finely chopped
2 large onions, peeled and thinly sliced
3 tbsp olive oil
75g/3oz stoned dried figs, finely chopped
1 tbsp soft, dark brown sugar
1 large green chilli, seeded and chopped
Juice of 2 limes
1 tsp tamarind paste

1 Cut the plums in half, remove the stones, then finely chop the flesh. Line a grill pan with a sheet of foil and preheat the grill.

2 Mix the sliced onions with the olive oil, place in the foil-lined pan and spread them out. Grill for 10 minutes, or until dark golden and softened.

3 Place the chopped plums in a large bowl with all the remaining ingredients and stir together. Add the hot onions to the bowl, stir and leave to stand for 1 hour.

4 Taste the salsa and season with salt and pepper. Pack into small clean jars and store in the refrigerator for up to 1 week.

Tip

Tamarind paste is sold in small tubs in delicatessens and supermarkets and adds a special mellow, sour flavour. It is very concentrated and has a strong flavour, so do not be tempted to use too much.

Uncooked Freezer Jam

Freezer friendly

Uncooked jams can be made from raspberries or strawberries and are set with liquid pectin. This is an ideal way to preserve smaller amounts of fresh fruit and, as these jams do not involve any heating or boiling, the fruit retains all its delicious flavour.

Ingredients
Makes 1.5kg/3lb

700g/1½lb raspberries, hulled

700g/1½lb caster sugar
2 tbsp lemon juice
125ml/4fl oz liquid pectin

1 Place the raspberries in a large non-metallic bowl. Crush the fruit lightly with a vegetable masher.

2 Stir in the sugar and lemon juice and leave to stand at room temperature for about 2 hours, until the sugar has completely dissolved. Stir the mixture occasionally.

3 Add the pectin and stir gently for a minute to mix thoroughly. Pour the jam into small, plastic, freezer-proof containers, allowing 2.5cm/1in head space at the top for the jam to expand on freezing.

4 Cover and leave to set for 24 hours. Press on lids or cover with cling wrap or foil and freeze the pots. To use, thaw at room temperature for 1-2 hours. It will keep for 6 months frozen.

Tip
Once you have defrosted the jam you will need to keep it stored in the refrigerator in a lidded container or jar.

Raspberry Iced Creams

Freezer friendly

Fresh raspberries have such an intense flavour that it is a shame to destroy it by cooking them. This easy iced dessert has only three ingredients and really captures the delicate taste of this luscious berry fruit.

Ingredients for 2

175g/6oz raspberries
3 tbsp golden icing sugar
150ml/¼pt extra-thick
    double cream
6 fresh raspberries,
    to garnish
Fresh mint sprigs,
    to garnish

Ingredients for 4

350g/12oz raspberries
6 tbsp golden icing sugar
300ml/½pt extra-thick
    double cream
12 fresh raspberries,
    to garnish
Fresh mint sprigs,
    to garnish

1 Remove any leaves or stalks from the raspberries, place them on a tray and open freeze for 30 minutes or until solid.

2 Place the frozen raspberries in a processor or liquidiser with the icing sugar and process for a few seconds, until the fruit resembles large crumbs.

3 Place the cream in a bowl and fold in the frozen crushed fruit. Place in a plastic freezer box and freeze for 30 minutes or until semi solid. Line 2 (4) small ramekins with cling wrap, pressing the film into all the corners.

4 Mash the ice cream with a fork to break up the ice crystals. Spoon into the ramekins and smooth the tops level. Freeze for a further 30 minutes or until needed. To serve, upturn the ramekins onto serving plates, lift away the ramekins and peel away the film wrap. Stand for 15 minutes to thaw slightly, then decorate with fresh raspberries and mint sprigs.

Red Fruit Compote

Freezer friendly

If you have currant bushes in your garden, you will find this fruit freezes well and you will be glad of a store of this easy-to-make dessert in your freezer. It is delicious served with ice cream and wafer biscuits and, with a minimum of cooking, the flavours are captured in these rich red juices.

Ingredients for 2

50g/2oz blackcurrants
50g/2oz redcurrants
1 tbsp medium white wine or
**   unsweetened apple juice**
25g/1oz granulated sugar
100g/4oz raspberries, hulled
Mint sprigs, to serve

Ingredients for 4

100g/4oz blackcurrants
100g/4oz redcurrants
2 tbsp medium white wine or
**   unsweetened apple juice**
50g/2oz granulated sugar
225g/8oz raspberries, hulled
Mint sprigs, to serve

1 Strip the black- and redcurrants from their stalks by pulling them away with the tines of a fork and trim away the end pieces with scissors. Place the currants in a small pan with the wine or apple juice.

2 Cover the pan and simmer for 3-5 minutes until the fruit pops and begins to soften.

3 Stir in the sugar and simmer over a low heat until every grain of sugar has dissolved.

4 Stir the raspberries into the warm mixture, then pour into a bowl to cool for 30 minutes. Chill in the refrigerator for 3 hours before serving or freeze straight away.

Tip

To freeze, pour the cold mixture into a rigid polythene box and freeze. It will keep for 6 months. To use, thaw in the refrigerator for 3 hours.

Raspberry Trifles

super quick

Creamy homemade custard and tangy fresh raspberries straight from the garden make this quick desert extra-special.

Ingredients for 2

100g/4oz trifle sponge cakes
3 tbsp sweet sherry or
    Madeira wine
3 medium eggs
50g/2oz vanilla caster sugar
600ml/1pt milk
225g/8oz fresh raspberries,
    hulled
Chocolate sprinkles,
    to decorate

Ingredients for 4

225g/8oz trifle sponge cakes
6 tbsp sweet sherry or
    Madeira wine
6 medium eggs
100g/4oz vanilla caster sugar
1.2l/2pt milk
450g/1lb fresh raspberries,
    hulled
Chocolate sprinkles,
    to decorate

1 Cut the sponge cakes into small pieces and place in a large bowl. Sprinkle over the sherry or wine and leave to stand for 10 minutes.

2 Beat the eggs and sugar together in a bowl with 3 (6) tbsp milk until smooth. Bring the remaining milk to the boil, remove from the heat and leave to stand for 5 minutes.

3 Gradually pour the hot milk over the egg mixture, whisking constantly until blended. Strain into the pan and heat gently, stirring, until the custard thickens and coats the back of a spoon. Do not allow the mixture to boil, which will cause it to separate.

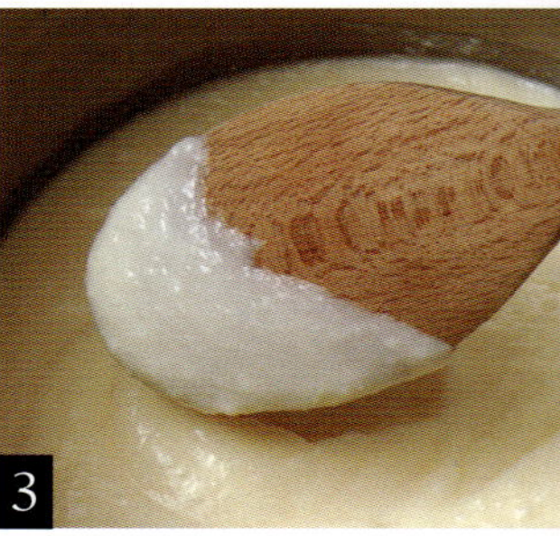

4 Cool the custard for 5 minutes. In 2 (4) tall glasses or dishes place layers of raspberries, sponge and cooled custard. Chill for 15 minutes before serving. Decorate with chocolate sprinkles.

Tip

Not suitable for freezing.

Rhubarb and Orange Chutney

Family favourite

If you have been put off making chutney because of the cooking aromas, try this easy version made in small amounts in the microwave oven.

Ingredients

575g/1¼lb fresh rhubarb, washed, trimmed and roughly chopped
225g/8oz onions, finely chopped
225ml/8fl oz white wine vinegar
100g/4oz sultanas
225g/8oz soft light brown sugar
2.5cm/1in piece fresh root ginger, peeled and grated
1 clove garlic, peeled and crushed
1 small green chilli, seeded and chopped

1 Place all the ingredients in a large microwave- and heat-proof bowl. Cook for 8 minutes on a high setting until the sugar has dissolved, stirring 3 times.

2 Continue to cook on a high setting for 15 minutes, uncovered, until the mixture is thick and well reduced. Stir twice in the first 10 minutes, then every following minute. Use oven gloves to hold the bowl and be very careful with the mixture in the last 5 minutes of cooking, because it will be very hot.

3 After 5 minutes, pour into warmed sterilised jars and cover with waxed discs while still hot. When cool, cover and label. Store for 3 months before using, to allow the flavour to develop.

4 To make the chutney on the hob, place all the ingredients in a large heavy-based saucepan. Simmer over a low heat for 5 minutes, stirring, until the sugar has dissolved. Raise the heat and cook for about 20 minutes, stirring occasionally, until the mixture is thick and pulpy.

Tip

These timings are based on a 750-watt microwave oven. If your oven has a higher or a lower power level you will need to adjust the timings and cook for a little longer or for less time.

Scottish Rhubarb Crumble

Family favourite

If you have a rhubarb patch, choose young thin sticks with a pretty pink colouring to the stems. If they pull away easily from the plant, they are ready for picking.

Ingredients for 2

350g/12oz rhubarb, washed
1 tbsp orange marmalade
40g/1½oz Demerara sugar
1 tbsp whisky
50g/2oz plain flour
40g/1½oz butter
40g/1½oz Demerara sugar
25g/1oz porridge oats
   or muesli

Ingredients for 4

700g/1½lb rhubarb, washed
2 tbsp orange marmalade
75g/3oz Demerara sugar
2 tbsp whisky
100g/4oz plain flour
75g/3oz butter
75g/3oz Demerara sugar
50g/2oz porridge oats
   or muesli

1 Preheat the oven to 180°C/350°F/gas mark 4. Butter a shallow ovenproof dish.

2 Trim the rhubarb and cut into 2.5cm/1in pieces. Stir together with the marmalade and sugar and place in the base of the dish. Sprinkle over the whisky.

3 Make the topping. Sift the flour into a bowl or food processor and rub in, or process, the butter until it resembles fine crumbs. Stir in the sugar and oats or muesli.

4 Sprinkle the crumble over the top of the rhubarb and bake for 30-35 minutes, until the top is golden and the fruit bubbles up around the edges.

Tip

For variety, use peeled, cored and chopped apples, halved and stoned plums or trimmed blackcurrants instead of rhubarb.

Rhubarb and Raspberry Jam

Perfect preserves

Rhubarb has a tart flavour but when it is combined with the sweeter raspberries, it makes a delicious jam. If fresh raspberries are not in season, you can make this preserve with frozen ones.

Ingredients
Makes 2.7kg/6lb

900g/2lb pink rhubarb, washed and chopped
150ml/¼pt water

500g/1lb 2oz raspberries, hulled
1.5kg/3lb granulated sugar
A small knob of butter

1 Trim the rhubarb and chop into 2.5cm/1in chunks. Place the rhubarb in a large heavy-based pan or a preserving pan and cook with the water for 10 minutes, until the fruit is soft and broken up.

2 Add the raspberries and cook for about 30 minutes or until the fruit is tender and the contents of the pan have reduced.

3 Remove from the heat and add the sugar. Cook over a low heat, stirring until every grain of the sugar has dissolved.

4 Add a small knob of butter and raise the heat to a boil. Boil rapidly for about 10 minutes until setting point has been reached (see plate test, page 22). Take the pan off the heat and remove any scum from the top of the jam with a metal spoon. Pour into warm, sterilised jars (see page 23), cover with waxed discs, wax side down and cover with lids and label when cool.

Tip
Home-frozen fruits can be used directly from the freezer, still in their icy state. If you cannot find raspberries you can use tayberries or loganberries instead.

Easy Strawberry Jam

Perfect preserves

Crushing the strawberries to soften the fruit instead of cooking them means they keep their delicious sweet flavour. Make sure the fruit is ripe enough to crush but not soft or mushy.

Ingredients
Makes 1.8kg/4lb

1kg/2lb strawberries
Juice of 1 lemon

1kg/2lb jam sugar
with pectin

1 Remove the hulls from the strawberries, rinse and dry the fruit. Place the berries in a bowl and crush lightly to a coarse pulp with a vegetable masher.

2 Place the crushed fruit in a large saucepan with the lemon juice. Warm over a medium heat until boiling. Reduce the heat to a simmer and cook over a low heat for 5 minutes until tender.

3 Remove the pan from the heat and add the sugar. Stir over a low heat until the grains of sugar have dissolved.

Raise the heat to a boil and boil for about 5 minutes until setting point has been reached (see plate test, page 22).

4 When the jam has reached setting point, remove the pan from the heat and skim away any scum from the top of the jam. Leave to stand for 5 minutes then pour into warmed, sterilised jars (see page 23). Stir the jam in the jars to distribute the fruit then cover with waxed discs, wax side down, cool completely then cover with cellophane tops and lids. Label and store in a cool, dark place.

Tip

Do not be tempted to overcook the jam: it will eventually go a dark brown colour and lose its setting qualities.

Strawberry and Mango Mousse Layers

Delicious desserts

The fresh flavour of sweet strawberries blends beautifully with ripe juicy mangoes in this easy, make-ahead dessert.

Ingredients for 2

2 tsp powdered gelatine
100ml/3½fl oz crème fraîche
1 small ripe mango
50g/2oz caster sugar
175g/6oz strawberries, hulled
2 tsp lemon juice
150ml/¼pt whipping cream

Ingredients for 4

4 tsp powdered gelatine
200ml/7fl oz crème fraîche
1 large ripe mango
100g/4oz caster sugar
350g/12oz strawberries, hulled
1 tbsp lemon juice
300ml/½pt whipping cream

1 Sprinkle the gelatine over 1 (2) tbsp water in a small bowl and leave to stand until the gelatine becomes spongy. Stand the bowl in a pan of warm water and heat gently to dissolve. Stir into the crème fraîche.

2 Peel the mango and slice the flesh away from the stone. Place the mango flesh in a food processor and purée with half the sugar until smooth.

3 Purée the strawberries with the lemon juice and remaining sugar.

4 Stir half the crème fraîche mixture into the mango purée and half into the strawberry purée. Whip the cream until it forms soft peaks then fold half into each mixture. Layer the two mixtures in tall glasses or in a large bowl. Chill for 30 minutes until set.

Tip

Not suitable for freezing.

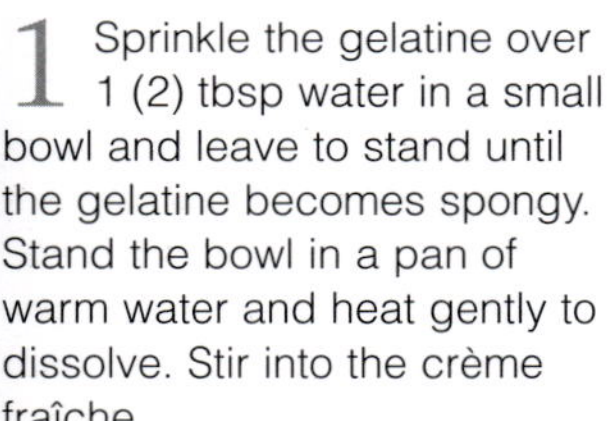

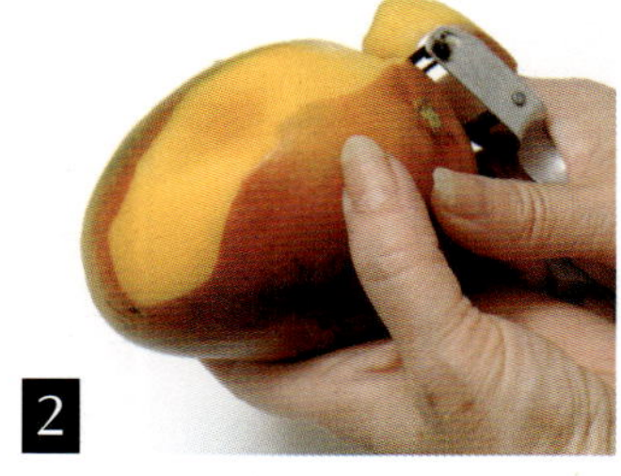

Quick Strawberry Dessert Sauce

Easy entertaining

Make a stock of this bright red tangy sauce for your freezer. It will add a touch of sunshine and bring plain ice cream or meringues to life in the winter months.

Ingredients
Makes 300ml/1/2pt

450g/1lb ripe strawberries, washed

75g/3oz icing sugar
1½ tbsp lemon juice
1 tbsp Cointreau or framboise liqueur (optional)

1 Remove the hulls from the strawberries and place the fruit in a food processor or liquidiser with the icing sugar and lemon juice.

2 Process the strawberries until smooth. If you do not have a food processor, mash the strawberries into a smooth pulp with a vegetable masher.

3 Strain the sauce through a fine sieve or a piece of muslin then add the liqueur if using.

Tip

To freeze, pour the sauce into small plastic bags or plastic freezer boxes. Label and use within 1 year. To use, thaw at room temperature for 3 hours until thoroughly defrosted.

Variations

Use 450g/1lb raspberries or blackcurrants instead of strawberries. Sieve the sauce through a fine mesh, as these fruits have quite a lot of pips.

French Strawberry Tart

Delicious desserts

Impress your guests with this glazed patisserie tart, packed with sweet, red summer fruits, but do not tell them you cheated by using shop-bought pastry and custard!

Ingredients
Makes a 23cm/9in tart

350g/12oz ready-made shortcrust pastry
1 egg, beaten
11g sachet powdered gelatine

250ml/8fl oz can or carton of ready-made vanilla dairy custard
500g/1lb 2oz strawberries, hulled
4 tbsp redcurrant jelly
3 tbsp fresh orange juice

1 Preheat the oven to 180°C/350°F/gas mark 4. Roll out the pastry thinly to line a 23cm/9in loose-based flan tin and prick with a fork. Chill in the freezer for 5 minutes.

2 Fill the pastry case with a sheet of non-stick baking paper and baking beans. Place on a baking sheet and bake for 10 minutes. Remove the paper and beans and brush inside the base and sides with beaten egg. Bake for a further 10 minutes until golden, then cool on a wire rack.

3 Place the orange juice in a small bowl, sprinkle over the gelatine and leave to become spongy. Dissolve in the microwave on a low setting or stand the bowl in a small pan of water and heat until dissolved. Stir the dissolved gelatine into the custard.

4 Remove the cooled pastry case from the flan tin and place on a serving plate. Spoon in the custard, smooth level, and chill for 30 minutes until set. Slice the strawberries and arrange in an overlapping pattern on top of the custard layer. Warm the redcurrant jelly until softened, then brush over the fruit. Chill for 20 minutes before serving.

Tip

To freeze, bake the pastry base, fill with custard, cool and cover with foil. Keeps for 3 months. Thaw at room temperature for 2 hours, then add the fruit topping and glaze.

vegetables

Asparagus and Cheese Tarts

Vegetarian

If you have an asparagus bed, you can look forward to a delicious harvest every year in the early summer months. These dainty little tarts capture the unique flavour and texture of this delicate vegetable. Serve them as a starter or as a luxury addition to a picnic.

Ingredients
Makes 10

225g/8oz plain flour
A pinch of salt
A pinch of cayenne pepper
100g/4oz chilled butter
25g/1oz Parmesan cheese,
    finely grated

Filling

350g/12oz fresh asparagus
    stems, trimmed
15g/½oz butter
2 shallots, finely chopped
100g/4oz Cheddar cheese,
    coarsely grated
3 medium eggs
225ml/ 8fl oz single cream
1 tbsp fresh chopped chives
Salt
Freshly ground black pepper

1 To make the pastry, sift the flour, salt and cayenne pepper into a bowl or a food processor. Rub or blend in the butter until it resembles fine crumbs. Stir in the Parmesan cheese and add enough chilled water to mix to soft dough. Wrap in cling wrap and freeze for 5 minutes.

2 Preheat the oven to 200°C/400°F/gas mark 6. Roll the pastry thinly and line ten greased 10cm/4in tartlet tins. Prick the bases of the tarts and line with greaseproof paper. Fill with baking beans and bake for 10 minutes. Remove the paper and beans and bake for a further 10 minutes.

3 Cut the asparagus stems into 2cm/¾in lengths, keeping the tips separate. Cook the stem pieces in 5cm/2in water in a small pan for 5 minutes then add the tips and cook for 23 minutes, until firm but just cooked. Drain.

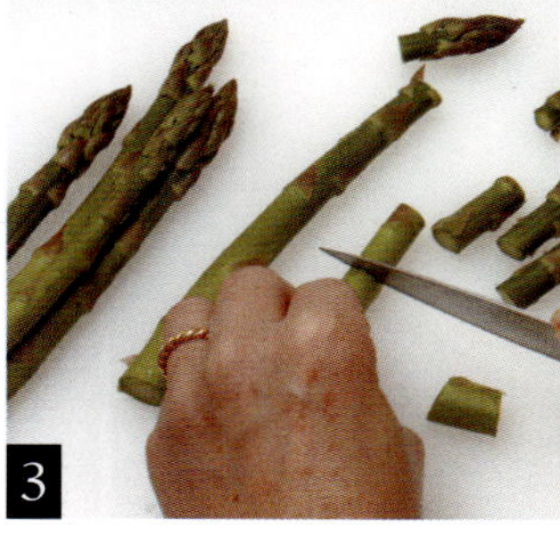

4 Heat the butter and fry the shallots until softened, 2-3 minutes. Scatter the asparagus, shallots and Cheddar cheese into the pastry cases. Whisk the eggs with the cream, chives and seasoning and carefully pour into the pastry cases. Bake for 15-20 minutes, or until the tops are golden and the filling is firm.

Pasta with Asparagus and Salmon

Low Fat

With its pale green colour, fresh asparagus blends beautifully with light pink salmon to make this pasta supper – ideal for easy entertaining.

Ingredients for 2

- 150g/5oz tagliatelle
- 100g/4oz asparagus, trimmed
- 1 tbsp dry white vermouth
- 75g/3oz low-fat fromage frais
- 3 tbsp single cream
- ½ tsp lemon juice
- 100g/4oz ready-cooked salmon pieces, flaked
- 15g/½ oz butter
- Snipped chives, to serve

Ingredients for 4

- 275g/10oz tagliatelle
- 225g/8oz asparagus, trimmed
- 2 tbsp dry white vermouth
- 175g/6oz low-fat fromage frais
- 6 tbsp single cream
- 1 tsp lemon juice
- 225g/8oz ready-cooked salmon pieces, flaked
- 25g/1oz butter
- Snipped chives, to serve

1 Cook the tagliatelle in a large pan of boiling salted water, according to pack instructions, drain and keep warm.

2 Cut the asparagus stems into 2cm/¾in lengths and keep the tips separate. Place 5cm/2in water in a large saucepan, add salt and bring to the boil. Add the stem pieces and simmer for 5 minutes. Add the tips and simmer for 3 minutes until just tender. Drain and reserve 3 (6) tbsp of the cooking liquid.

3 Stir the vermouth, fromage frais, cream and lemon juice into the liquid and stir in the salmon pieces.

4 Gently toss the pasta in the butter with the asparagus pieces and divide between serving bowls. Serve the sauce over each bowl and sprinkle with snipped chives.

Tip

Not suitable for freezing.

Toasted Aubergine Salad

Easy entertaining

Aubergines are quite easy to grow, so you might be lucky enough to pick this vegetable straight from the garden and toast it into these delicious strips for a summer salad.

Ingredients

Serves 4 as a starter or 2 as a light meal

1 medium aubergine, trimmed
6 tbsp olive oil
1 tbsp balsamic vinegar
75g/3oz soft sun-dried tomatoes in oil, drained
100g/4oz feta or goats cheese, crumbled
175g/6oz mixed leaf salad

Dressing

4 tbsp olive oil
1 tbsp white wine vinegar
1 tsp French mustard
A pinch of caster sugar
Salt
Freshly ground black pepper

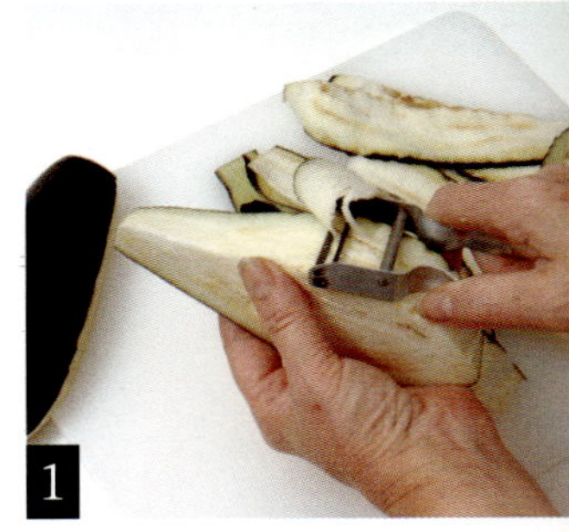

1 Cut the aubergine flesh into very thin long slices. You can do this by cutting down one side of the aubergine with a potato peeler.

2 Whisk the oil and vinegar together in a large bowl and toss the aubergine slices in the mixture.

3 Lightly oil a heavy-based griddle pan with vegetable oil and heat to hot. If you do not have a griddle, use a grill pan. Cook the aubergine slices in batches over a high heat for half a minute on each side until tender and toasted.

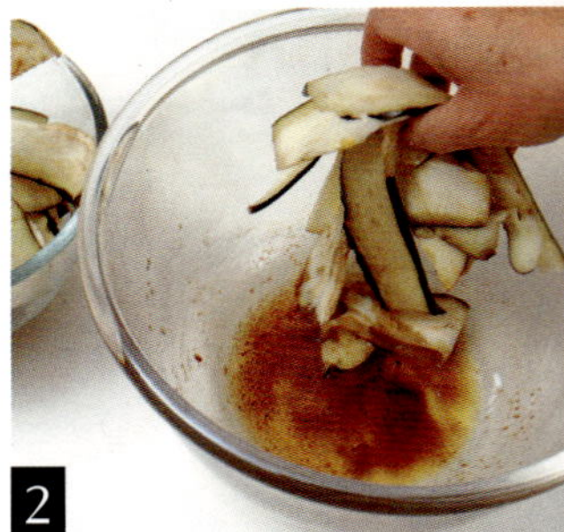

4 Arrange the slices on serving plates with the sun-dried tomatoes, crumbled feta cheese and salad leaves. To make the dressing, whisk the oil, vinegar and mustard together with the seasonings and drizzle over the top just before serving.

Variation

You can combine the aubergine slices with olives, char-grilled peppers or artichokes in oil (drained) or ripe beefsteak tomatoes, thinly sliced.

Ratatouille-filled Pasta Rolls

Vegetarian

All the ingredients for ratatouille – aubergines, courgettes, onions peppers and tomatoes – are stuffed into these delicious pasta rolls.

Ingredients
Serves 4

12 lasagne sheets or cannelloni tubes (225g/8oz)
75g/3oz Cheddar cheese, grated

Sauce

1 tbsp olive oil
1 medium onion, peeled and chopped
1 clove garlic, peeled and chopped
400g/14oz can chopped tomatoes
1 tbsp chopped fresh basil
1 tsp balsamic vinegar
A pinch of sugar

Filling

1 large aubergine
2 large courgettes, trimmed
1 large red pepper, cored and halved
1 large onion, peeled
1 clove garlic, peeled and crushed
1 tbsp olive oil
Salt
Freshly ground black pepper
1 tbsp pesto

1 Preheat the oven to 220°C/425°F/gas mark 7. Grease a 400ml/14fl oz (800ml/1½pt) shallow ovenproof dish. Start with the filling. Chop the aubergine, courgettes, red pepper and onion into small dice and place in a roasting dish. Toss with the oil and garlic and season with salt and pepper.

2 Roast for 30 minutes or until the vegetables are tender. Place in a bowl to cool and stir together with the pesto sauce.

3 Meanwhile, make the sauce. Heat the oil and fry the onion and garlic for 5 minutes to soften. Add the tomatoes and stir over a low heat then add the basil and balsamic vinegar and season with salt, pepper and sugar. Place in a food processor and blend until smooth. Return to the pan with 300ml/½pt water.

4 If using dried lasagne sheets, place in boiling water for 2-3 minutes to soften, then drain. Divide the vegetable filling between them and roll them up or stuff the cannelloni tubes. Place in the dish and spoon the sauce over them. Sprinkle over the cheese. Reduce the oven temperature to 200°C/400°F/gas mark 6 and bake for 25 minutes or until the pasta is tender and the top is golden and bubbling.

Tip

To freeze, cook and cool the dish and freeze in the serving dish. Keeps for 4 months. To use, thaw for 4 hours and reheat for 20 minutes at 180°C/350°F/gas mark 4 or in the microwave oven, according to your oven's instruction manual.

Beetroot and Walnut Salad

vegetarian

Beetroots are easy to grow and it is a real pleasure to pull a few plants from the ground and cook them straight away to reveal their delicious sweet flavour. You will find the flavours of beetroot and walnuts blend beautifully together in this salad.

Ingredients for 2

175g/6oz bunch of raw beetroot with stalks
1 tsp cider vinegar
1 tsp caster sugar
1 sprig fresh thyme
1 bay leaf
1 clove garlic
40g/1½oz walnuts
1½ tbsp olive oil
1 tbsp walnut oil
1 tsp cider vinegar
Salt
Freshly ground black pepper
Mixed salad leaves with rocket, to serve
50g/2oz goats cheese, or soft cheese such as Brie, diced, to serve

Ingredients for 4

350g/12oz bunch of raw beetroot with stalks
1 tbsp cider vinegar
2 tsp caster sugar
1 sprig fresh thyme
1 bay leaf
2 cloves garlic
75g/3oz walnuts
3 tbsp olive oil
2 tbsp walnut oil
1 tbsp cider vinegar
Salt
Freshly ground black pepper
Mixed salad leaves with rocket, to serve
100g/4oz goats cheese, or soft cheese such as Brie, diced, to serve

1 Wash the beetroots thoroughly, leaving them unpeeled with the stalks and roots attached and place them on a large sheet of foil that will fit inside a large saucepan.

2 Sprinkle with the vinegar and sugar and add the thyme, bay leaf and garlic. Bring the sides of the foil up and fold over to form a sealed parcel. Pour enough water into the pan to come halfway up the sides of the parcel. Simmer the beetroot for about 30 minutes or until tender. Larger beetroots will take longer than small ones.

3 Remove the parcel from the pan. Open the foil and reserve 1 tbsp (2 tbsp) of the cooking liquid. Drain the beetroots and, when cool enough, rub away the skins and trim the stalks off.

4 Dry-fry the walnuts in a non-stick frying pan for 1 minute to improve their flavour. Chop the nuts finely and place in a bowl, Slice the beetroot and place in the bowl.

5 To make the dressing, whisk the oils, vinegar and cooking liquid together with salt and freshly ground black pepper, add to the bowl and toss together. Chill until completely cold.

6 Serve with salad leaves and diced soft cheese.

Tip

The salad will keep chilled in the refrigerator for up to 2 weeks.

Borsch

Family favourite

You will find different versions of borsch all over Eastern Europe. Some contain strips of beef or ham, and are served as a complete meal. This version makes a hearty supper served with chunks of crusty bread.

Ingredients for 2

600ml/1pt beef stock
115g/4oz raw beetroot, washed
1 tsp red wine vinegar
12g/½oz butter
1 small clove garlic, peeled and chopped
1 onion, peeled and sliced
115g/4oz potatoes, peeled and cubed
115g/4oz cabbage, trimmed and shredded
1 carrot, peeled and sliced
1 tbsp tomato purée
½ tsp caster sugar
Salt
Freshly ground black pepper
2 tbsp soured cream
1 tbsp fresh chopped parsley

Ingredients for 4

1.2l/2pt beef stock
225g/8oz raw beetroot, washed
1 tbsp red wine vinegar
25g/1oz butter
1 clove garlic, peeled and chopped
2 onions, peeled and sliced
225g/8oz potatoes, peeled and cubed
225g/8oz cabbage, trimmed and shredded
2 carrots, peeled and sliced
2 tbsp tomato purée
1 tsp caster sugar
Salt
Freshly ground black pepper
4 tbsp soured cream
2 tbsp fresh chopped parsley

1 Place the stock in a large heavy-based pan and heat gently. Peel and grate the beetroot and add to the stock. Add the vinegar and simmer for 20 minutes.

2 Melt the butter in a large pan and fry the garlic and onions lightly for 2-3 minutes to soften. Add the potatoes, cabbage and carrots and fry for a further minute. Add all the vegetables to the pan with the stock.

3 Add the tomato purée, season the soup with the sugar and salt and pepper. Bring to the boil then simmer, covered with a lid, for 40 minutes or until the vegetables are tender.

4 Pour into warmed serving bowls and add a tablespoon of soured cream to each one. Sprinkle with fresh chopped parsley to serve.

Tip

To freeze, cook and cool the soup and pack in strong freezer bags or boxes. It will keep for 3 months. To use, thaw at room temperature or in the microwave. Reheat in a saucepan or in the microwave until piping hot.

Broad Bean and Vegetable Lasagne Layer

Freezer friendly

If you have plenty of summer vegetables available, make a few batches of this easy supper dish for your freezer.

Ingredients for 2

75g/3oz carrots, sliced
2 small sticks celery, trimmed and chopped
1 small leek, sliced
115g/4oz shelled broad beans
12g/½oz butter
12g/½oz plain flour
150ml/¼pt semi-skimmed milk
75ml/2½fl oz vegetable stock
85g/3oz Cheddar cheese, grated
115g/4oz button mushrooms, sliced
115g/4oz sweet corn
Salt
Freshly ground black pepper
40g/1½oz no-cook lasagne

Ingredients for 4

175g/6oz carrots, sliced
3 sticks celery, trimmed and chopped
1 large leek, sliced
225g/8oz shelled broad beans
25g/1oz butter
25g/1oz plain flour
300ml/½pt semi-skimmed milk
150ml/¼pt vegetable stock
175g/6oz Cheddar cheese, grated
225g/8oz button mushrooms, sliced
225g/8oz sweet corn
Salt
Freshly ground black pepper
75g/3oz no-cook lasagne

1 Preheat the oven to 200°C/400°F/gas mark 6. Butter a shallow ovenproof dish. Place the carrots, celery, leek and broad beans in a large pan and cover with boiling water. Bring to the boil then simmer, covered, for 5 minutes until tender. Drain, reserving 75ml/2½fl oz (150ml/¼pt) of the vegetable stock.

2 Make the sauce. Melt the butter in a large pan, stir in the flour and cook, stirring for 1 minute. Gradually stir in the milk and vegetable stock, stirring constantly until the sauce has thickened. Stir in half the cheese, the cooked vegetables, mushrooms and sweet corn and season well with salt and pepper.

3 Place a layer of lasagne sheets in the base of the dish. Spoon over a layer of vegetable sauce, then continue layering the sauce and pasta, finishing with a layer of sauce.

4 Sprinkle over the remaining cheese and bake in the centre of the oven for 30 minutes, until the top is golden and bubbling.

Tip

To freeze, cook and cool the lasagne and leave in the serving dish. For four individual portions, freeze in the dish, cut into four frozen squares using a freezer knife and wrap individually. Keeps for 4 months. To use, thaw at room temperature and place in ovenproof dishes. Reheat at 180°C/350°F/gas mark 4 for 20 minutes or in the microwave oven according to your manufacturer's instructions.

Pasta Fagioli

Easy entertaining

For a quick and easy supper dish, serve fresh pasta topped with tasty bright green broad beans.

Ingredients for 2

225g/8oz broad beans,
250g/9oz stuffed pasta such
  as tortellini with cheese
  and walnuts
300ml/½pt semi-skimmed
  milk
1 level tbsp cornflour
25g/1oz Parmesan cheese,
  grated
40g/1oz Parma ham, sliced
  into thin strips
1 tbsp fresh basil, chopped
Freshly ground black pepper

Ingredients for 4

450g/1lb broad beans
500g/1lb 2oz stuffed pasta,
  such as tortellini with
  cheese and walnuts
600ml/1pt semi-skimmed
  milk
2 level tbsp cornflour
50g/2oz Parmesan cheese,
  grated
75g/3oz Parma ham, sliced
  into thin strips
2 tbsp fresh basil, chopped
Freshly ground black pepper

1 Shell the broad beans and parboil for 4-5 minutes until tender, and drain. If the beans are young leave the skins on, if they are old and large, slip away the grey outer skins while the beans are warm.

2 Cook the pasta in a large pan of boiling salted water according to pack instructions, drain and keep warm.

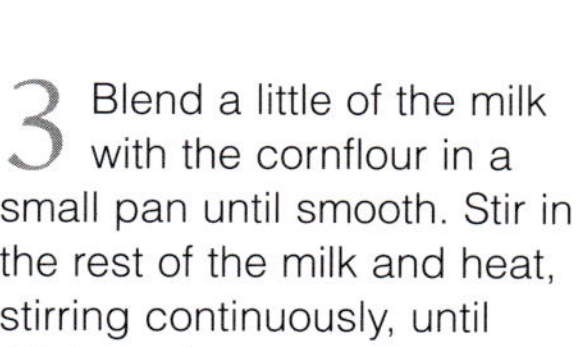

3 Blend a little of the milk with the cornflour in a small pan until smooth. Stir in the rest of the milk and heat, stirring continuously, until thickened.

4 Add the broad beans and the cheese and cook for 2 minutes then stir in the ham and basil. Season with freshly ground black pepper. Do not add any salt as the Parma ham will be salty enough.

Tip

Not suitable for freezing.

Spicy Carrot and Coriander Soup — *Freezer friendly*

Turn your home-grown carrots into this delicious fresh and creamy soup, which also makes a great stand-by for the freezer.

Ingredients for 2

15g/½oz butter
1 small onion, peeled
   and chopped
450g/1lb young carrots,
   trimmed and grated
1 stick celery, finely chopped
600ml/1pt hot vegetable stock
Finely grated rind of ½ orange
Salt
Freshly ground black pepper
150ml/¼pt crème fraîche
2 tbsp fresh coriander
   leaves, chopped

Ingredients for 4

25g/1oz butter
1 large onion, peeled
   and chopped
1kg/ 2lb young carrots,
   trimmed and grated
2 sticks celery, finely chopped
1.2l/2pt hot vegetable stock
Finely grated rind of 1 orange
Salt
Freshly ground black pepper
300ml/½pt crème fraîche
3 tbsp fresh coriander
   leaves, chopped

1 Melt the butter in a large, pan and add the onions. Cook over a low heat for 3 minutes, until transparent.

2 Add the carrots and celery and stir together for 2 minutes, then add the stock and bring to the boil. Reduce to a simmer and cover the pan.

3 Simmer over a low heat for about 30 minutes or until the carrots are tender. Cool for 10 minutes then place in a blender or food processor and blend until smooth.

4 Return the soup to the pan. Add the grated orange rind, salt, pepper, crème fraîche and half the coriander and gently reheat. Spoon into warmed bowls and serve sprinkled with the remaining chopped coriander.

Tip

If you cannot get fresh coriander, use 1 tbsp each of chives, watercress and parsley. To freeze, cool and pack into strong freezer bags or boxes. The soup keeps for 6 months.

Turkish Carrot Salad

vegetarian

If you have plenty of carrots in the garden, try this bright salad with its crisp and crunchy texture. Serve it with crusty bread and a selection of vegetable salads or to accompany cold sliced beef, ham or chicken.

Ingredients for 2

Juice of ½ lemon
3 tbsp olive oil
1 tbsp clear honey
¼ tsp ground cinnamon
A pinch of salt
Freshly ground black pepper
6mm/¼in piece fresh root
    ginger, peeled
350g/12oz young carrots,
    peeled and trimmed
25g/1oz sultanas
Lettuce leaves, to serve

Ingredients for 4

Juice of 1 lemon
6 tbsp olive oil
2 tbsp clear honey
½ tsp ground cinnamon
¼ tsp salt
Freshly ground black pepper
1cm/½in piece fresh root
    ginger, peeled
700g/1lb young carrots,
    peeled and trimmed
50g/2oz sultanas
Lettuce leaves, to serve

1 Make the dressing first. Mix the lemon juice, oil, honey, cinnamon, salt and pepper together in a small bowl. Finely grate the ginger into the bowl. Whisk everything together.

2 Grate the carrots coarsely by hand or in a food processor.

3 If you want to prepare the salad ahead, place the dressing separately in a sealed jar and store the carrots in cold water until needed,

4 To serve, toss the carrots in the dressing with the sultanas and place on a bed of lettuce leaves.

Tip

Store the salad for up to one week in a sealed container in the refrigerator. Not suitable for freezing.

Passion Cake

Freezer friendly

There are many versions of carrot cake or passion cake as it is called in Europe. This one has plenty of carrots, which add a delicious sweetness when combined with cinnamon and hazelnuts.

Ingredients
Serves 12

225g/8oz carrots, peeled and trimmed
225g/8oz soft margarine
225g/8oz soft, light brown sugar
4 medium eggs, beaten
100g/4oz wholewheat flour
100g/4oz plain flour
1 tsp ground cinnamon
2 tsp baking powder

50g/2oz ground hazelnuts
75g/3oz raisins
1 tbsp milk

Frosting

175g/6oz full-fat, soft, cream cheese
175g/6oz icing sugar
1 tsp orange or lemon juice
Fine strips of orange or lemon peel

1 Preheat the oven to 180°C/350°F/gas mark 4. Grease and line a 20cm/8in round spring-clipped cake tin with non-stick baking paper. Finely grate the carrots.

2 Place the margarine, sugar and eggs in a bowl and sift in the flours, cinnamon and baking powder, adding any bran from the sieve.

3 Beat for 2 minutes, then stir in the grated carrots, hazelnuts and raisins with enough milk to make a soft mixture. Spoon into the tin and make a hollow in the centre of the cake with the back of a spoon.

4 Bake for 1 hour 15 minutes or until well risen and firm to the touch. Cool in the tin for 10 minutes then turn onto a wire rack. Beat the cream cheese, icing sugar and juice together for the frosting. Spread over the top and sides of the cake and scatter the strips of rind over the top.

Mustard Pickle

Store-cupboard special

Mustard pickles, sometimes called piccalilli, are a great way of using up a glut of summer vegetables from the garden. You can enjoy this colourful, spicy pickle later in the year or at Christmas – it makes a perfect partner for cold meats.

Ingredients
Makes 2.3kg/5lb

1 small cauliflower, outer leaves removed
450g/1lb young tender marrow, peeled and seeded
1 cucumber
225g/8oz runner beans
450g/1lb small pickling onions
1 red pepper, halved and cored
100g/4oz salt
50g/2oz plain flour
15g/½oz turmeric
1 tsp ground ginger
50g/2oz mustard powder
225g/8oz golden caster sugar
1.2l/2pt distilled spiced malt vinegar

1 Cut the cauliflower into small florets. Chop the marrow into small chunks. Chop the cucumber into small chunks. String the runner beans and chop into 2.5cm/1in lengths. Peel and trim the onions, dice the red pepper.

2 Layer the vegetables in a large non-metallic bowl and sprinkle each layer with 1-2 tbsp salt. Sprinkle the top layer with salt and cover with a plate. Leave to stand for 24 hours in a cool place.

3 Place the flour, spices, mustard powder and sugar in a large saucepan. Blend to a paste with a little of the vinegar, then blend in the remaining vinegar. Stir over a low heat until the sauce thickens.

4 Rinse the vegetables thoroughly and drain. Add to the pan with the sauce and bring to the boil before simmering for 10-15 minutes until the vegetables are still firm. Turn off the heat and spoon the vegetables into sterilised, warmed jars (see page 23). Take care to distribute the different vegetables evenly. Pour enough sauce into each jar to cover the vegetables, cool, then seal and label. Store in a cool place for 1 month before use to allow the flavours to mellow.

Celery and White Bean Soup

vegetarian

This hearty soup is a great way of using up celery and any spare vegetables from the garden. It makes a filling supper dish, served with chunks of crusty bread.

Ingredients for 2

1 small leek, cleaned
12g/½oz butter
1 small clove garlic, chopped
1 carrot, peeled
1 small head of celery, washed
1 tsp plain flour
375ml/10fl oz vegetable stock
Finely grated zest of
½ lemon
200g/7oz can butter or
cannellini beans, drained
1 tsp chopped
flat-leaf parsley
Salt
Freshly ground black pepper

Ingredients for 4

1 leek, cleaned
25g/1oz butter
1 clove garlic, chopped
2 carrots, peeled
1 head of celery, washed
1 tbsp plain flour
750ml/1¼pt vegetable stock
Finely grated zest of
½ lemon
400g/14oz can butter or
cannellini beans, drained
1 tbsp chopped
flat-leaf parsley
Salt
Freshly ground black pepper

1 Thinly slice the leek into rings. Melt the butter in a deep, heavy-based pan and fry the leeks with the chopped garlic for 3-4 minutes to soften.

2 Chop the carrots and celery into slices. Add to the pan and stir for 2-3 minutes. Sprinkle over the flour and stir again to coat the vegetables.

3 Add the stock and lemon zest and bring to the boil, stirring until slightly thickened. Cover and simmer for 30 minutes or until the vegetables are tender.

4 Stir in the beans, parsley and season to taste. Simmer the soup for 5 minutes to heat the beans.

Tip

Cool the soup, then freeze in individual bags of one or two portions for easy serving. The soup will keep for 3 months.

Celeriac Remoulade

Easy entertaining

Celeriac is a knobbly root vegetable with a mild celery flavour. Harvest it in the late autumn and winter months for shredding into soups and salads. This creamy vegetable salad is delicious served with sliced beef and baby new potatoes and is ideal to serve on a cold buffet table.

Ingredients for 2

2 tsp sunflower oil
½ tbsp yellow mustard seeds
1 tbsp French mustard
½ tsp white wine vinegar
25g/1oz mayonnaise
3 tbsp soured cream
Salt
Freshly ground black pepper
350g/12oz head of celeriac
25g/1oz gherkins, sliced
   into strips
2 tsp flat-leaf parsley

Ingredients for 4

1 tbsp sunflower oil
1 tbsp yellow mustard seeds
2 tbsp French mustard
1 tsp white wine vinegar
50g/2oz mayonnaise
5 tbsp soured cream
Salt
Freshly ground black pepper
700g/1¼lb head of celeriac
50g/2oz gherkins, sliced
   into strips
1 tbsp flat-leaf parsley

1 Heat the oil in a pan and add the mustard seeds. Cover with a lid and cook until the seeds pop, then pour them into a bowl.

2 Stir in the mustard, vinegar, mayonnaise and soured cream, and season with salt and ground black pepper.

3 Peel the celeriac and grate it finely by hand or in a food processor using the grating blade.

4 Fold the celeriac into the dressing and scatter with the sliced gherkins and parsley. Chill in the refrigerator for 1 hour before serving. It will keep for 1-2 weeks, chilled.

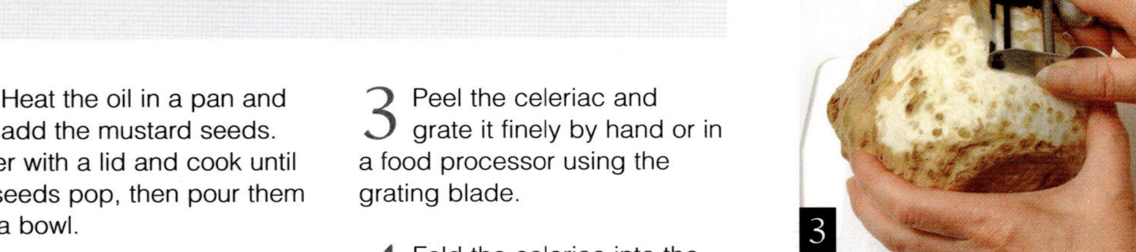

Tip

Not suitable for freezing.

Courgette Tea Bread

For the cake tin

Grated courgettes keep this dark tea bread sticky and moist. Serve it sliced and buttered and keep any extra in the cake tin for up to a week, if it lasts that long!

Ingredients
Makes a 900g/2lb loaf

1 large egg
125ml/4fl oz sunflower oil
175g/6oz courgettes, wash and trimmed
150g/5oz wholewheat flour

½ tsp baking powder
1 tsp bicarbonate of soda
1 tsp ground cinnamon
175g/6oz soft, dark brown sugar
75g/3oz sultanas
75g/3oz walnuts, chopped

1 Preheat the oven to 180°C/350°F/gas mark 4. Grease and line the base of a 900g/2lb loaf tin with non-stick baking paper.

2 Beat the egg and sunflower oil together in a jug. Grate the courgettes into a large bowl, using a medium-sized grating blade.

3 Sift the flour, baking powder, bicarbonate of soda and spices into the bowl and stir in the sugar, sultanas

and walnuts. Pour in the oil and egg from the jug and mix to a thick batter. Pour into the prepared tin.

4 Bake for about 1 hour, or until a skewer inserted into the centre comes out cleanly. Cool in the tin for 10 minutes then turn out to cool on a wire rack. Store in a cool place for up to 1 week.

Tip

To freeze, bake, cool and wrap the cake tightly in foil. It will keep for 2 months. Leftover slices can be frozen, separated and wrapped in cling wrap. To use, defrost at room temperature for 2 hours. Cut the cake with a very sharp knife as it will be moist and sticky.

Green Vegetable Curry with Courgettes

vegetarian

This curry is based on just fresh green vegetables. Serve it with a dish of dhal, or to accompany chicken or meat curries with rice or Indian breads.

Ingredients for 2

1 tbsp sunflower oil
1 medium onion, chopped
1cm/½in piece root ginger, peeled and grated
1 small clove garlic, chopped
3 cardamom pods, crushed
3 whole cloves
2 tbsp natural yoghurt
40g/1½oz green lentils, washed
300ml/½pt vegetable stock
80g/3oz potatoes, peeled and cubed
100g/4oz leaf spinach
100g/4oz courgettes, sliced
¼ small cauliflower, broken into florets
50g/2oz peas
1 small green chilli, seeded and sliced

Ingredients for 4

2 tbsp sunflower oil
1 large onion, chopped
2.5cm/1in piece root ginger, peeled and grated
1 clove garlic, chopped
6 cardamom pods, crushed
5 whole cloves
4 tbsp natural yoghurt
75g/3oz green lentils, washed
600ml/1pt vegetable stock
175g/6oz potatoes, peeled and cubed
225g/8oz leaf spinach
225g/8oz courgettes, sliced
½ small cauliflower, broken into florets
100g/4oz peas
1 green chilli, seeded and sliced

1 Heat the oil in a large pan, add the onion and fry for 2 minutes to soften. Add the ginger, garlic, cardamom pods, and cook for 2 minutes.

2 Add the cloves, yoghurt and lentils and stir together. Pour in the vegetable stock, cover and cook over a low heat for 30 minutes, until the lentils are softened.

3 Parboil the potatoes for 10 minutes then drain and add to the pan. Add the remaining ingredients and bring to the boil.

4 Cover and simmer for 10-15 minutes until the vegetables are tender. Serve with rice and poppadums.

Blue Cheese and Broccoli Soup

Freezer friendly

If you have Stilton cheese left over after the Christmas season, combine it with some fresh broccoli from the garden to make this delicious warming soup.

Ingredients for 2

225g/8oz fresh broccoli, washed
12g/½oz butter
1 medium onion, peeled and chopped
1 stick celery, trimmed and chopped
1 tsp plain flour
300ml/½pt hot vegetable stock
A pinch grated nutmeg
Salt
Freshly ground black pepper
150ml/¼pt milk
40g/1½oz Stilton or hard blue cheese, crumbled
Croutons and celery leaves to garnish

Ingredients for 4

450g/1lb fresh broccoli, washed
25g/1oz butter
1 large onion, peeled and chopped
2 sticks celery, trimmed and chopped
1 tbsp plain flour
600ml/1pt hot vegetable stock
¼ tsp grated nutmeg
Salt
Freshly ground black pepper
300ml/½pt milk
75g/3oz Stilton or hard blue cheese, crumbled
Croutons and celery leaves to garnish

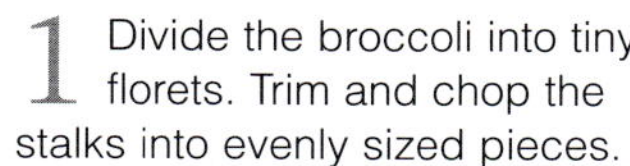

1 Divide the broccoli into tiny florets. Trim and chop the stalks into evenly sized pieces.

2 Heat the butter in a large, heavy-based pan and fry the onion and celery over a low heat for 5 minutes to soften the vegetables. Do not brown them. Add the broccoli and cook for a further 2 minutes.

3 Stir in the flour and toss the vegetables to coat them. Add the hot stock and stir well. Bring to the boil, then turn down the heat. Season with nutmeg, salt and pepper. Cover and simmer for 15 minutes until the vegetables are tender.

4 Cool slightly then place the soup in a food processor or liquidiser and process until smooth. Wash out the pan and return the soup to it. Add the milk and the crumbled cheese and heat gently until the cheese has melted. Do not allow the soup to boil or the cheese will become stringy. Serve immediately with crispy bread croutons and celery leaves.

Tip

To freeze, cook and cool the soup and pack into strong freezer bags or boxes. It will keep 3 months. To use, thaw or place frozen blocks in a saucepan or in the microwave and gently defrost.

Making Croutons

To make croutons, slice off the crusts from two slices of bread and cut the bread into small cubes. Heat 15g/1oz butter with 1 tsp sunflower oil in a small frying pan and fry the bread, stirring frequently, until dark golden brown.

Broccoli and Cheese Tart

vegetarian

If you have a vegetarian to feed, it need not be a problem as this is a recipe that all the family will enjoy as well. This tart freezes well, so make a stock for the freezer if you have a glut of broccoli in your garden.

Ingredients
Makes a 23cm/9in tart

175g/6oz plain flour
75g/3oz vegetable margarine
25g/1oz Parmesan cheese, finely grated
10g/4oz carrots, thinly sliced

225g/8oz small broccoli florets
100g/4oz vegetarian red Leicester cheese, crumbled
3 medium eggs
225ml/8fl oz milk
25g/1oz flaked almonds

1 Preheat the oven to 200°C/400°F/gas mark 6. Grease a 23cm/9in fluted flan dish. Make the pastry. Place the flour in a bowl with the margarine and rub in until the mixture resembles fine crumbs. Stir in the grated Parmesan and about 2 tbsp cold water enough to mix to a soft dough. Wrap and freeze for 5 minutes, or chill for 1 hour.

2 Cook the carrots in a large pan of boiling salted water for 3 minutes. Add the broccoli and cook for a further 2 minutes. Drain and refresh under cold running water.

3 Roll out the pastry to a circle large enough to line the flan dish. Prick the base with a fork, fill with greaseproof paper and baking beans and bake blind for 15 minutes. Remove the paper and beans and bake for another 5 minutes.

4 Layer the carrots, and broccoli in the case. Scatter the cheese over. Beat the eggs and milk together and pour into the flan. Top with the nuts and bake for about 45 minutes, until golden and firm in the centre. Serve hot or cold with salads.

Tip

To freeze, cool the tart and wrap tightly in foil. It will keep for 3 months. To use, remove the foil and thaw at room temperate for 3 hours or on a defrost setting in the microwave oven.

Bread-and-butter Pickles

Store-cupboard special

This is an ideal way to use up a glut of summer cucumbers. These tart, crisp pickles are great served with hot, fried fish dishes or with cold sliced ham.

Ingredients
Makes 1.8kg/4lb

1.2l/2pt white distilled vinegar
1 tbsp pickling spice
3 bay leaves

175g/6oz granulated sugar
2 cucumbers, each weighing about 575g/1¼lb
700g/1lb onions
1 large green pepper
50g/2oz tbsp salt

1 Put the vinegar, pickling spice, bay leaves and sugar in a bowl and place over a pan of hot water. Cook, stirring, over a medium heat for 10 minutes, remove from the heat, cover the bowl and leave to stand for 24 hours to infuse the flavours.

2 Peel the cucumber and slice into 5cm/2in pieces, then quarter each piece. Peel and thinly slice the onions. Remove the core and seeds from the pepper and slice thinly.

3 Put the vegetables in a bowl in layers and sprinkle each layer with salt. Leave to stand for 2 hours in a cool place. Rinse the vegetables under cold running water, then drain and dry thoroughly.

4 Pack the dry vegetables into large, sterilised jars (see page 20). Strain the vinegar into a jug and pour over the vegetables to cover them. Cover with a vinegar-proof seal and label. Keep the pickle for 2 weeks in a cool place to develop the flavours before using.

Tip
This will keep for 3 months in a cool dark place. Not suitable for freezing.

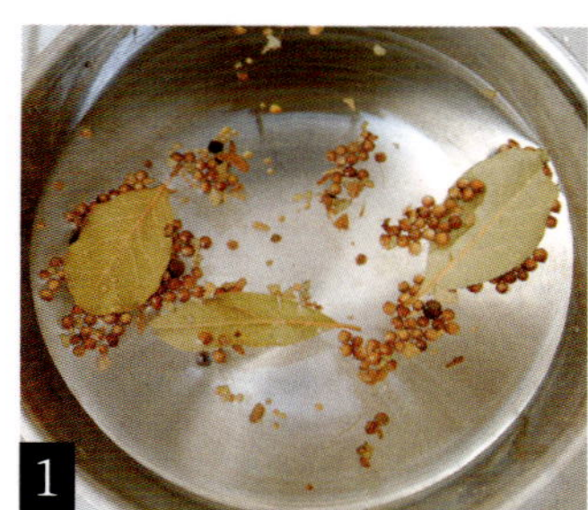

Chilled Cucumber and Yoghurt Soup

Easy entertaining

Chilled soups are so refreshing on a hot summers day. This one is uncooked and retains all the natural taste of fresh cucumber.

Ingredients for 2

1 medium cucumber, washed
225g/8oz thick Greek yoghurt
1 clove garlic, peeled
**   and chopped**
150ml/¼pt water
1 tsp olive oil
½ tsp white wine vinegar
2 tbsp fresh mint
2 tbsp chives, snipped
Salt
White pepper
Fresh mint and melba toast,
**   to serve**

Ingredients for 4

1 large cucumber, washed
450g/llb thick Greek yoghurt
2 cloves garlic, peeled
**   and chopped**
300ml/½pt water
2 tsp olive oil
1 tsp white wine vinegar
4 tbsp fresh mint
4 tbsp chives, snipped
Salt
White pepper
Fresh mint and melba toast,
**   to serve**

1 Cut the cucumber in half lengthways without peeling. Take a teaspoon and scoop out the seeds from each half. Roughly chop the cucumber into large chunks.

2 Place the cucumber in a food processor or blender with the yoghurt, garlic, 150ml/¼pt water, oil, vinegar and 1 tbsp (2 tbsp) each of the mint and chives.

3 Blend to a purée, then pour into a bowl, cover and chill for 1 hour.

4 Taste the soup and season with salt and white pepper, then fold in the remaining mint and chives. If the soup is very thick add a little more water. Garnish with fresh mint, and serve with crisp melba toasts.

Tip

Pack into freezer bags to freeze. Defrost at room temperate and whisk before serving if the soup has separated. It will keep for 2 months.

Florence Fennel with Bacon and Cheese

Easy entertaining

The flavours of cream, nutmeg and cheese go perfectly with the slight liquorice flavour of fennel. Serve this dish as a main course or, if you want to serve it as a side dish, omit the bacon.

Ingredients for 2

225g/9oz large bulbs of fennel, trimmed
Sea salt
1 tsp olive oil
40g/½oz streaky or back bacon, rinded and chopped
3 tbsp crème fraîche
A small pinch of freshly grated nutmeg
25g/1oz Cheddar cheese, grated

Ingredients for 4

500g/1lb 2oz large bulbs of fennel, trimmed
Sea salt
2 tsp olive oil
75g/3oz streaky or back bacon, rinded and chopped
6 tbsp crème fraîche
A pinch of freshly grated nutmeg
50g/2oz Cheddar cheese, grated

1 Slice the fennel bulbs thickly. Place in a saucepan and pour over 150ml/¼pt (300ml/½pt) water and sprinkle with salt.

2 Bring to the boil and simmer for 20-25 minutes, until the fennel feels tender.

3 Remove the fennel with a slotted spoon and place in a buttered, shallow heatproof dish, overlapping the slices. Boil the cooking water rapidly until it reduces by two thirds.

4 Heat the oil in a small pan and fry the bacon until crisp. Scatter over the fennel in the dish. Blend the crème fraîche with the cooking liquid and add the nutmeg. Sprinkle over the cheese and grill for 3-4 minutes, until the cheese is melted and golden.

Tip

To freeze, cool and sprinkle with grated cheese, but do not grill. Freeze in the cooking dish, covered with foil. It will keep for 3 months. Defrost and reheat in the microwave or in the oven (180°C/350°F/gas mark 4) for 20 minutes, then grill to brown.

Homemade Pesto Sauce

something special

If you have never tasted fresh pesto, made from your own herbs, you have missed one of life's great pleasures. Grow plenty of basil next summer and try making your own version of this Italian delicacy.

Ingredients
Serves 4

2 cloves of garlic
100g/4oz fresh basil leaves
3 tbsp pine nuts

Coarse sea salt
50g/2oz Parmesan cheese,
    freshly grated
8 tbsp extra virgin olive oil
45g/ 1½oz butter, softened

1 Lightly bruise the garlic cloves with the blade of a heavy knife, crushing them just enough to loosen the skin.

2 Lightly wash the basil leaves in cold water, being careful not to bruise them. Drain and pat dry with kitchen paper.

3 Place the basil, garlic, pine nuts and a pinch of sea salt in a mortar. Using a round movement, grind all the ingredients against the side of the mortar until they have been ground to a paste.

4 Scoop into a bowl and add the grated cheese. Trickle the olive oil into the mixture in a thin stream, beating into the herb mixture. When all the oil has been added, beat in the butter until smooth. Store chilled in a small jar until needed.

5 To use, blend the pesto with 1 tbsp hot water to dilute it slightly and toss into hot, cooked spaghetti or tagliatelle.

6 To make the pesto in a food processor, place the garlic, basil, pine nuts, oil and salt in a food processor and blend until smooth. Add the cheese, process, then add the butter and process again.

Tip

To freeze, make the pesto using the processor method, but do not add the cheese or butter. Pack in small lidded tubs and it will keep for 2 months. Thaw at room temperature then add the cheese and butter and process until smooth.

Italian Herb-stuffed Chicken Breasts

Easy entertaining

These chicken breasts are packed with the taste of summer herbs. Prepare them ahead of time to make an easy main course for a supper party.

Ingredients for 2

15g/½ oz butter
1 shallot, finely chopped
1 slice Parma ham,
    finely chopped
1 tbsp white breadcrumbs
15g/½oz Parmesan cheese,
    finely grated
1 tbsp each fresh chopped
    basil and parsley
2 chicken breasts, boned
Salt
Freshly ground black pepper
1 tbsp olive oil
2 tbsp crème fraîche
1 tbsp fresh pesto

Ingredients for 4

25g/1 oz butter
2 shallots, finely chopped
2 slices Parma ham,
    finely chopped
2 tbsp white breadcrumbs
50g/1oz Parmesan cheese,
    finely grated
2 tbsp each fresh chopped
    basil and parsley
4 chicken breasts, boned
Salt
Freshly ground black pepper
2 tbsp olive oil
4 tbsp crème fraîche
2 tbsp fresh pesto

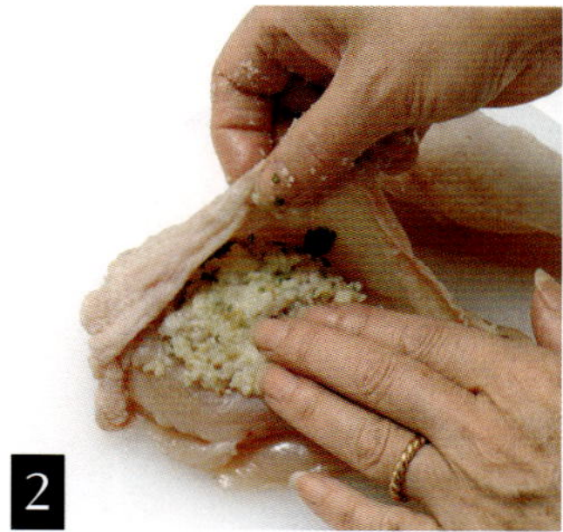

1 Preheat the oven to 200°C/400°F/gas mark 6. Make the stuffing. Melt the butter and fry the chopped shallots for 2-3 minutes to soften.

2 Cool slightly then stir the Parma ham, breadcrumbs, Parmesan and herbs. Mix to a soft paste. Loosen the skin from the chicken, leaving one side attached. Divide the stuffing into 2 (4) portions and stuff under the skin. Pull the skin over the stuffing, season with salt and pepper and brush lightly with olive oil.

3 Place in a roasting tin and bake for 20–25 minutes until they are golden brown and cooked through.

4 To make the sauce, whisk the crème fraîche with the juices in the roasting pan until hot and smooth. Whisk in the pesto and remove from the heat. Serve the chicken sliced on plates with the sauce drizzled over.

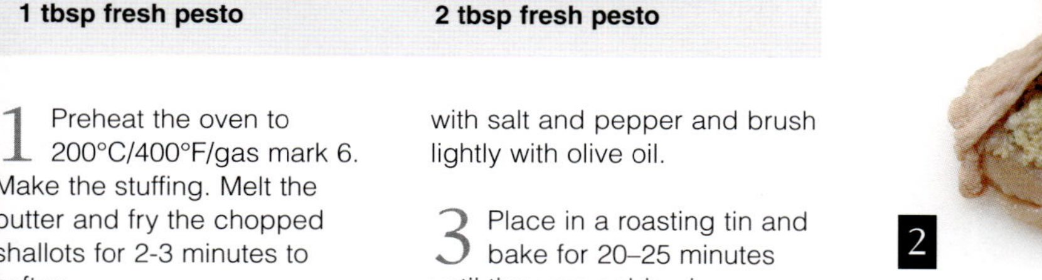

Creamy Leek and Potato Soup

Family favourite

This hearty soup is a great way to use up winter root vegetables and is popular with adults and children alike. Make a stock for the freezer so that you always have a wholesome supper dish to hand.

Ingredients for 2

1 leek, trimmed
15g/½oz butter
350g/12oz old potatoes, peeled
300ml/½pt hot vegetable stock
Salt
Freshly ground black pepper
45ml/1½fl oz cream
Fresh chives, chopped, and croutons, to serve

Ingredients for 4

2 leeks, trimmed
25g/1oz butter
700g/1½lb old potatoes, peeled
600ml/1pt hot vegetable stock
Salt
Freshly ground black pepper
90ml/3fl oz cream
Fresh chives, chopped, and croutons, to serve

1 Cut the leeks halfway down to the root and wash well by swirling in plenty of cold water to remove grit between the leaves. Slice the leeks finely.

2 Melt the butter in a large pan. Add the leeks. Cook over a low heat for 3 minutes, without allowing them to brown.

3 Chop the potatoes roughly and add to the pan. Stir with the leeks, add the vegetable stock and bring to the boil. Simmer, covered for 30 minutes, or until tender.

4 Remove from the heat and cool for 5 minutes, then place in a food processor and blend in batches until smooth. Return to the pan, season, and reheat to just below boiling. Turn off the heat and add the cream. Serve sprinkled with chopped chives and croutons (see page 178).

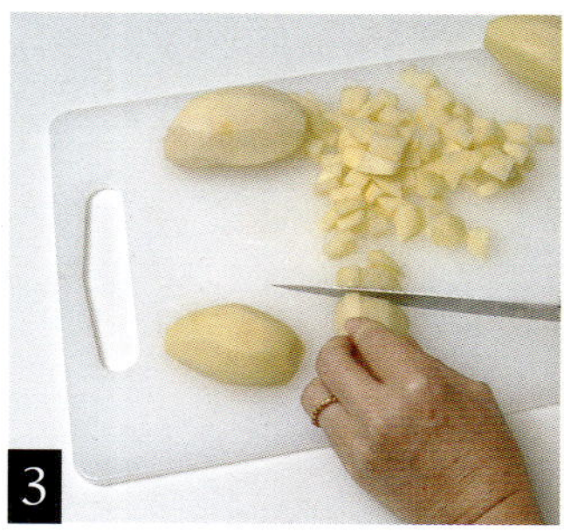

Tip

To freeze, cook and cool the soup and pack into rigid polythene bags or boxes. It will keep for 9 months. To use, thaw at room temperature, heat and adjust the seasoning if necessary.

Cheesy Leeks and Ham

super quick

Leeks are at their best in the late autumn and freshly dug leeks have a unique flavour and fragrance. Try this quick-and-easy supper dish for a warming family meal and you will find it soon becomes a favourite.

Ingredients for 2

**2 medium leeks (about
    25cm/10in length),
    trimmed and washed**
2 slices lean ham
15g/½oz butter
15g/½oz plain flour
225ml/8fl oz milk
½ tsp French mustard
**40g/1½oz Cheddar cheese,
    grated**
Salt
White pepper
**15g/½oz fresh brown
    breadcrumbs**

Ingredients for 4

**4 medium leeks (about
    25cm/10in length),
    trimmed and washed**
4 slices lean ham
40g/1oz butter
40g/1oz plain flour
450ml/¾pt milk
1 tsp French mustard
**75g/3oz Cheddar cheese,
    grated**
Salt
White pepper
**25g/1oz fresh brown
    breadcrumbs**

1 Preheat the oven to 200°C/400°F/gas mark 6. Slice each leek in half and cook in a large pan of salted boiling water for 3-4 minutes until just tender. Drain well.

2 Cut the ham slices in half, then wrap round the leeks. Arrange as a single layer in a shallow ovenproof dish.

3 Make the sauce. Melt the butter in a medium pan, remove from the heat and add the flour. Stir until the mixture has a sandy consistency.

Return to the heat and gradually whisk in the milk until smooth. Bring to the boil, stirring constantly until the sauce is thick and smooth.

4 Add the mustard and 25g/1oz (50g/2oz) of the cheese and season with salt and white pepper, then pour over the leeks. Mix the remaining cheese and breadcrumbs together and sprinkle over the dish. Bake for 20 minutes until the topping is crisp and golden.

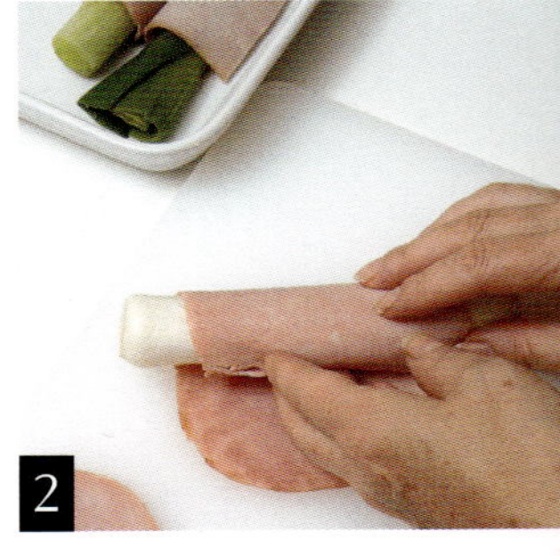

Stuffed Marrow

Family favorite

If you have grown lots of marrows, try this family meal, stuffed with a meaty sauce. It is very cheap and easy to make.

Ingredients for 2

- 1 small marrow weighing about 450g/1lb
- 1 tsp sunflower oil
- 1 small onion, finely chopped
- 100g/4oz lean minced beef
- 1 medium carrot, peeled and chopped
- 50g/2oz button mushrooms, chopped
- 1 tbsp tomato purée
- ½ tsp Worcestershire sauce
- 75ml/2½fl oz beef stock
- ½ tsp dried mixed herbs

Ingredients for 4

- 1 large marrow weighing about 900g/2lb
- 1 tbsp sunflower oil
- 1 medium onion, finely chopped
- 225g/8oz lean minced beef
- 2 medium carrots, peeled and chopped
- 100g/4oz button mushrooms, chopped
- 2 tbsp tomato purée
- 1 tsp Worcestershire sauce
- 150ml/¼pt beef stock
- 1 tsp dried mixed herbs

1 Preheat the oven to 190°C/350°F/gas mark 5. Peel the marrow with a potato peeler. Cut the marrow in half lengthways.

2 Scoop out the seeds from the centre of the marrow with a dessert spoon, making a deep hollow cavity in each side.

3 Heat the oil in a large pan and fry the onion for 4 minutes to soften. Add the minced beef and stir-fry until the meat has browned, about 5 minutes. Add all the remaining ingredients and bring to the boil. Stir, cover and simmer for 15 minutes, until thickened.

4 Place the marrow on a sheet of foil and fill the cavity of one half with the hot filling. Heap up the filling and place the other half of the marrow on top. Wrap completely in foil and bake for 50 minutes – 1 hour until the marrow is tender.

Tip Not suitable for freezing.

Microwaved Marrow with Tomatoes

Quick and Easy

Marrow served as a vegetable accompaniment can be rather bland. Mixing it with a stronger flavour, such as tomato, works very well.

1 small marrow, weighing about 450g/1lb
150ml/¼pt passata
½ tsp dried oregano or dried mixed herbs
Salt
Freshly ground black pepper

1 large marrow, weighing about 900g/2lb
300ml/½pt passata
1 tsp dried oregano or dried mixed herbs
Salt
Freshly ground black pepper

1 Peel away the thick skin from the outside of the marrow with a potato peeler. Cut the marrow into 2.5cm/1in thick slices. Cut the slices in half lengthways, scoop out the seeds and throw them away.

2 Place the slices flat in a buttered microwave-proof dish, arranging them so that they fill out all the spaces.

3 Heat the passata to just below boiling, stir in the herbs and pour the mixture over the marrow slices in the dish. Season with salt and freshly ground black pepper.

4 Cover the dish with cling wrap and cook on a high setting for 6 minutes, turning the dish halfway through cooking. Test to see if the marrow slices are tender. If not cook for another 30 seconds and test again.

5 To cook in a conventional oven, preheat the oven to 190°C/350°F/gas mark 5. Place the marrow slices in an ovenproof dish, pour over the tomato mixture and cover with foil. Bake for 35-45 minutes, until the marrow is tender.

Sprinkle 50g/2oz grated Cheddar cheese on the finished dish and cook under a hot grill for 1-2 minutes, until melted and bubbling.

Caramelised Shallot Marmalade

Perfect preserves

This confit is aromatic, with a sweet-and-sour flavour. It is delicious served with rich dishes containing fat, such as paté, roast duck or pork dishes.

Ingredients
Makes 225g/8oz

500g/1lb 2oz shallots, peeled
4 tbsp olive oil
1 tbsp unsalted butter
1 strip of lemon zest
1 cinnamon stick

2 dried chillies
4 whole cloves
2 cardamom pods, crushed
225g/8oz granulated sugar
½ tsp freshly ground black pepper
6 tbsp sherry vinegar

1 Slice the shallots into thick rings. Heat the oil and butter in a deep, heavy-based pan and add the shallot slices. Cook over a very low heat for 15 minutes to soften, until golden.

2 Place the lemon zest, cinnamon, chillies, cloves and cardamom pods in a square of muslin and tie up with string.

3 Add the bag of spices and the sugar to the shallots. Stir until the sugar has dissolved, then simmer for 40-50 minutes, stirring regularly.

4 Add the pepper and vinegar and simmer for another 15 minutes until the mixture is thick, brown and sticky. Remove the bag of spices and store the marmalade in a small lidded jar or container. It will keep for up to 1 week chilled.

Tip

Place in small lidded containers to freeze. It will keep for 2 months. To use, thaw at room temperature for 1 hour. Stir well before serving.

Baked Stuffed Onions

Family favourite

If you grow large Spanish onions, they are far too good just for chopping. Use them for stuffed onions, which are excellent on their own as a light meal or served with roasted meats. For a vegetarian version, omit the bacon.

Ingredients for 2

2 large firm onions weighing about 225g/8 oz each
1 tbsp wholewheat breadcrumbs
15g/½oz unsalted butter, chopped into small pieces
25g/1oz walnuts, chopped
50g/2oz streaky bacon, trimmed and finely chopped
40g/1½oz blue cheese such as Stilton or Roquefort
Salt
Freshly ground black pepper
1 tsp Worcestershire sauce
2 tsp olive oil

Ingredients for 4

4 large firm onions weighing about 225g/8 oz each
2 tbsp wholewheat breadcrumbs
25g/1oz unsalted butter, chopped into small pieces
50g/2oz walnuts, chopped
100g/4oz streaky bacon, trimmed and finely chopped
75g/3oz blue cheese such as Stilton or Roquefort
Salt
Freshly ground black pepper
2 tsp Worcestershire sauce
4 tsp olive oil

1 Preheat the oven to 190°C/375°F/gas mark 4. Lightly oil a shallow ovenproof baking dish. Place the whole onions, unpeeled, in a pan of water. Bring to the boil, simmer for 5 minutes, then drain and rinse under cold running water.

2 Trim away the ends and cut each onion in half, crosswise. Peel away the skins and scoop out the centres from each half, leaving a 6mm/¼in thick shell.

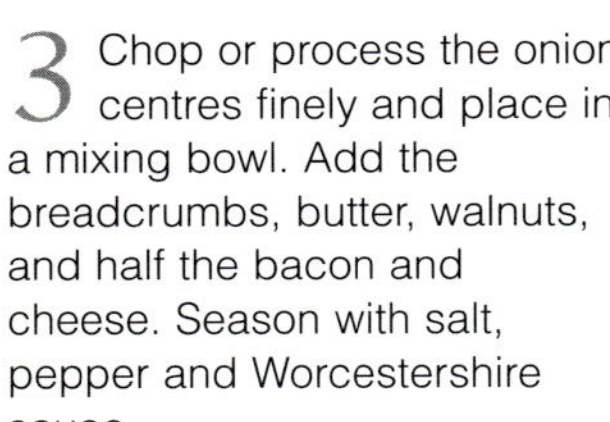

3 Chop or process the onion centres finely and place in a mixing bowl. Add the breadcrumbs, butter, walnuts, and half the bacon and cheese. Season with salt, pepper and Worcestershire sauce.

4 Fill each onion half with the mixture and sprinkle over the remaining bacon and cheese. Drizzle with olive oil and bake for 30 minutes until golden and bubbling.

Red Onion and Mushroom Tart

vegetarian

Red onions are always worth growing as they have a good firm texture and a mild but interesting flavour. They are delicious grilled or added to quiches.

Ingredients
Makes a 20cm/8in tart

100g/4oz plain flour
100g/4oz wholewheat flour
A pinch of salt
100g/4oz butter or block
   margarine
1 tbsp sunflower oil
75g/3oz chestnut
   mushrooms

2 medium red onions, peeled
1 tbsp chopped flat-leaf
   parsley
1 tbsp chopped fresh basil
2 medium eggs
200ml/6fl oz milk
75g/3oz vegetarian Cheddar
   cheese, grated
Salt
Cayenne pepper

1 Make the pastry. Sift the flours and salt into a bowl or food processor. Add the butter or margarine, cut into small pieces. Rub or process the fat into the flour until it forms soft crumbs. Add about 4 tbsp cold water and stir until a soft ball forms. Wrap the pastry in cling wrap and chill for 30 minutes.

2 Preheat the oven to 200°C/400°F/gas mark 6. Grease a 20cm/8in flan ring or tin and place on a baking sheet. Roll out the chilled pastry to form a 30cm/12in circle. Line the tin with the pastry and cover the base and sides with a sheet of greaseproof paper. Fill with dried baking beans and bake blind for 15 minutes. Remove the paper and beans and turn the oven down to 180°C/350°F/gas mark 4.

3 Chop the onions coarsely and quarter the mushrooms. Fry the onions in the oil for 5 minutes to soften, stir in the mushrooms and cook for 3 minutes. Place in the pastry case and sprinkle over the herbs.

4 Beat the eggs with the milk and 50g/2oz of the cheese. Season with salt and cayenne pepper and pour over the filling in the pastry case. Sprinkle the remaining cheese over the top and bake for 20 minutes or until the filling has set and the top is golden.

Pickled Onions

Store-cupboard special

Crunchy, home-made pickled onions are a delightful treat served with bread and cheese or cold meats.

Ingredients
Makes 1.8kg/4lb

1.8kg/4lb small pickling onions
100g/4oz coarse salt

1.2l/2pt water
1.2l/2pt malt vinegar
25g/1oz pickling spice
Bay leaves

1 Trim a slice from the ends of each onion. Place them in a large bowl, pour over enough boiling water to cover them and leave to soak for 5 minutes. Drain and slip the skins away until all the onions have been peeled.

2 Mix the salt with 1.2l/2pt water to make a brine solution. Pour the brine over the onions to cover them and place a plate over to keep them below the surface. Leave to soak for 48 hours.

3 Put the vinegar and pickling spices in a non-metallic bowl and cover with a plate. Set the bowl over a pan of cold water and bring to the boil. Remove from the heat and leave to infuse and cool for 2 hours.

4 Strain the onions from the brine solution and rinse them thoroughly under cold running water. Drain until completely dry then place them in jars with a sprig of bay leaf in each jar. Pour away any drops of water that have settled in the jars. Pour the cold, spiced vinegar into the jars to cover the onions completely. Seal with an airtight seal and store for 3 months before using, to let the flavours blend and mellow.

Tip

Add 4 dried chillies to the vinegar infusion and 2 dried chillies to each jar instead of bay leaves. Keeps for 6 months.

Pork and Pak Choi Stir-fry

super quick

Pak choi is a very easy vegetable to grow and needs similar conditions to lettuce. The white part of pak choi is sweet and crunchy, while the green part melts to a velvety smoothness similar to spinach.

Ingredients for 2

100g/4oz pork fillet
2 tbsp clear honey
½ tbsp sunflower oil
1 spring onion, sliced
½ red pepper, seeded
    and sliced
1 clove garlic, peeled
    and crushed
100g/4oz pak choi
½ tbsp rice vinegar
1 tbsp soy sauce

Ingredients for 4

225g/8oz pork fillet
3 tbsp clear honey
1 tbsp sunflower oil
2 spring onions, sliced
1 red pepper, seeded
    and sliced
1 clove garlic, peeled
    and crushed
225g/8oz pak choi
1 tbsp rice vinegar
2 tbsp soy sauce

1 Cut the pork fillet into thin slices and toss in 1 tablespoon of the honey. Heat the oil in a large non-stick pan or wok, and fry the slices for 2-3 minutes until lightly browned. Remove from the pan with a slotted spoon and keep warm.

2 Add the onions, pepper and garlic to the pan and stir-fry for 2-3 minutes to soften. Separate the pak choi into leaves if the bunches are large, then add to the pan and stir-fry for 2-3 minutes.

3 Add the vinegar, soy sauce and remaining honey and simmer for 2 minutes until the green leaves begin to wilt.

4 Return the pork slices to the pan and stir together until thoroughly heated. Serve with boiled rice noodles.

Tip

Not suitable for freezing.

Parsnip and Apple Mash

Freezer friendly

If you grow parsnips you will probably be looking for new ways of cooking them other than roasting or adding to soups. This mash recipe makes the most of their sweet flavour, combines well with the tartness of apples, and is ideal for the freezer.

Ingredients for 2

350g/12oz parsnips,
    scrubbed and trimmed
100g/4oz dessert apples,
    peeled and cored
25g/1oz butter
½ medium egg yolk
½ tbsp clear honey
1 pinch cinnamon
Salt
Freshly ground black pepper
Fresh parsley, chopped

Ingredients for 4

700g/1lb parsnips,
    scrubbed and trimmed
225g/8oz dessert apples,
    peeled and cored
50g/2oz butter
1 medium egg yolk
1 tbsp clear honey
1 pinch cinnamon
Salt
Freshly ground black pepper
Fresh parsley, chopped

1 Cut the parsnips into thick slices. If they are old, cut away the woody core from the centre of each one.

2 Place the parsnips in a pan of salted, boiling water and cook for 10 minutes. Cut the apples into chunks. Add to the pan and cook for a further 5 minutes until the parsnips and apples are tender.

3 Drain the parsnips and apples, place in a bowl and mash roughly together with a vegetable masher. Wash the pan out and add the butter.

4 Over a low heat, beat the mash with the butter, egg yolk, honey and cinnamon then season with salt and pepper. Fold in the chopped parsley just before serving. Serve with roast chicken, pork, or grilled sausages.

Tip

Freeze the purée without the parsley in polythene freezer boxes. It will keep for 6 months. To use, thaw and fold in the parsley.

Roasted Parsnips with Honey and Ginger

Easy Entertaining

Roasted parsnips are delicious served with a crispy roast chicken or loin of pork. Try this tasty variation with mustard, honey and a tang of ginger.

Ingredients for 2

225g/½lb parsnips,
    scrubbed and trimmed
1 tbsp sunflower oil
1 tbsp whole-grain mustard
1 tbsp clear honey
1 tbsp fresh root ginger,
    finely grated

Ingredients for 4

450g/1lb parsnips,
    scrubbed and trimmed
2 tbsp sunflower oil
2 tbsp whole-grain mustard
2 tbsp clear honey
2 tbsp fresh root ginger,
    finely grated

1 Preheat the oven to 220°C/425°F/gas mark 7. Cut the parsnips into pieces about 8cm/3in long and 2.5cm/1in thick. If they are old and have thick woody cores, cut these out.

2 Heat the oil in a small roasting pan. Add the parsnips and cook quickly over a high heat, tossing in the pan to colour evenly.

3 Place the tray in the oven and roast for 10 minutes, shaking the pan occasionally.

4 Mix the mustard, honey and ginger together in a small bowl, tip the paste into the pan and stir to coat the parsnips. Bake for 5 minutes until the parsnips are golden and tender. Serve hot with grilled meats such as chicken or pork.

Tip

Not suitable for freezing.

Fresh Pea and Serrano Ham Soup

Freezer friendly

The flavour of fresh peas, straight from the garden, is always delicious. If you have plenty of fresh peas to spare, preserve this taste of summer in your freezer.

Ingredients for 2

450g/1lb peas in their shells
15g/½ oz Serrano ham
1 spring onion, trimmed
3 large lettuce leaves,
**   washed**
600/1pt vegetable stock
Salt
White pepper
1 tbsp double cream
1 tbsp fresh mint, chopped,
**   plus sprigs of mint**

Ingredients for 4

900g/2lb peas in their shells
25g/1oz Serrano ham
2 spring onions, trimmed
6 large lettuce leaves,
**   washed**
1.2ltrs/2pt vegetable stock
Salt
White pepper
2 tbsp double cream
1 tbsp fresh mint, chopped,
**   plus sprigs of mint**

1 Shell the peas and throw away the pods. Cut the ham into small cubes and slice the spring onions thinly. Chop the lettuce coarsely.

2 Place the peas, ham, onions and leaves in a large, heavy-based saucepan. Add the stock and season with salt and white pepper.

3 Bring to the boil, then simmer for 20 minutes, until the peas are softened.

4 Cool the soup slightly, then place in a blender or liquidiser and blend to a purée with the chopped mint. Add the cream and taste the soup, adding a little more seasoning if necessary. Serve hot or chill the soup and serve cold.

Tip

To freeze, cook and cool the soup and pack into strong freezer bags or boxes. It will keep 3 months. To use, thaw at room temperature or place blocks of soup in a saucepan and heat gently from frozen.

Mange-tout Stir-fry with Prawns

Quick and easy

Tender young mange-tout peas are delicious in stir-fries. Pick them straight from the plants to enjoy their marvellous fresh flavour.

Ingredients for 2

1 tbsp sunflower oil
1 clove garlic, peeled and
   chopped
1cm/½in piece fresh ginger,
   peeled and grated
175g/6oz peeled raw prawns
4 spring onions, trimmed
   and chopped
100g/4oz mange-tout peas
1 tbsp soy sauce
2 tsp cornflour
1 tbsp lemon juice
1 tsp caster sugar

Ingredients for 4

2 tbsp sunflower oil
2 cloves garlic, peeled and
   chopped
2.5cm/1in piece fresh ginger,
   peeled and grated
350g/12oz peeled raw prawns
8 spring onions, trimmed
   and chopped
225g/8oz mange-tout peas
2 tbsp soy sauce
1 tbsp cornflour
2 tbsp lemon juice
2 tsp caster sugar

1 Heat the oil in a large pan or wok and add the garlic and ginger and stir-fry for 1 minute.

2 Add the raw prawns and fry for 3-4 minutes, stirring constantly, until they change colour from grey to pink.

3 Add the spring onions and mange-tout and stir-fry for 2-3 minutes.

4 Blend the soy sauce, cornflour, lemon juice and sugar to a paste, then add 3 tbsp (6 tbsp) water. Pour into the pan and boil for a minute until the mixture thickens. Serve immediately with noodles or rice.

Tip

Not suitable for freezing.

Roasted Pepper Salad

vegetarian

Make the most of home-grown peppers in this easy salad. Serve it as a starter with other vegetable dishes, or with cold meats such as salami.

Ingredients for 2

½ red pepper, washed
½ green pepper, washed
½ yellow pepper, washed
1 tbsp fresh basil leaves
1 tsp fresh mint leaves
1 tbsp white wine vinegar
A pinch of caster sugar
A small pinch of sea salt
Ground black pepper
4 tbsp olive oil
Whole basil leaves, to serve

Ingredients for 4

1 red pepper, washed
1 green pepper, washed
1 yellow pepper, washed
2 tbsp fresh basil leaves
1 tbsp fresh mint leaves
2 tbsp white wine vinegar
½ tsp caster sugar
A pinch of sea salt
Ground black pepper
8 tbsp olive oil
Whole basil leaves, to serve

1 Place the whole peppers under a hot grill. Grill them for 4-6 minutes, turning, until they are blistered and browned all over.

2 Place the peppers in a plastic bag, seal the bag and leave the peppers to cool.

3 Make the dressing. Place the basil and mint leaves in a small food processor and process or chop finely. Add the vinegar, sugar, seasonings and oil and process or mix to a thick green dressing.

4 When the peppers are cool, open the plastic bag and pull the skins away. The steam will have loosened them. Halve the peppers, cut out the seeds and stalks and cut the flesh into strips. Place in a bowl and toss in the dressing. Serve garnished with basil leaves.

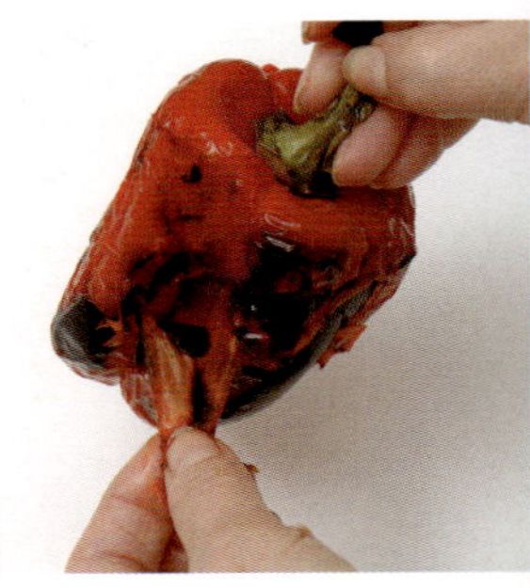

Tip

For a light lunch, serve sprinkled with toasted pine nuts, with crumbled feta cheese and a mixed rocket salad. Not suitable for freezing.

Spicy Hot Gazpacho Soup

Freezer friendly

Normally, gazpacho soup is served chilled, but this hot version really warms you up and clears a jaded palate.

Ingredients for 2	Ingredients for 4
1 tbsp olive oil	2 tbsp olive oil
1 medium onion, peeled and finely chopped	2 medium onions, peeled and finely chopped
1 clove garlic, peeled and chopped	2 cloves garlic, peeled and chopped
1 red chilli, seeded and finely chopped	2 red chillies, seeded and finely chopped
¼ tsp paprika	½ tsp paprika
1 carrot, grated	2 carrots, grated
1 stick celery, finely chopped	2 sticks celery, finely chopped
½ tsp ground cumin	1 tsp ground cumin
½ tsp ground coriander	1 tsp ground coriander
200g/7oz chopped canned tomatoes in juice	400g/14oz chopped canned tomatoes in juice
½ red pepper, seeded and chopped	1 red pepper, seeded and chopped
½ green pepper, seeded and chopped	1 green pepper, seeded and chopped
300ml/ ½pt vegetable stock	600ml/1pt vegetable stock
1 tbsp fresh coriander, chopped	2 tbsp fresh coriander, chopped
Salt	Salt
Freshly ground black pepper	Freshly ground black pepper

1 Heat the oil in a large, heavy-based saucepan and fry the onions, garlic and chillies for 5 minutes until softened but not browned.

2 Add the paprika, carrots, celery, ground cumin and coriander and stir together over a low heat for 2 minutes. Add the tomatoes and chopped peppers and stir together.

3 Pour in the stock and bring to the boil. Reduce the heat and simmer, covered, for 40 minutes.

4 Cool the soup for 10 minutes, then place in a liquidiser or processor and blend in batches until smooth. Rinse the pan and return the soup. Add the fresh chopped coriander and season to taste.

Tip

Freeze the cooled soup in strong freezer bags or boxes. It will keep for 6 months. To use, thaw at room temperature or place the frozen blocks in a saucepan and gently thaw on a low heat.

Fluffy Mash-topped Casserole

Family favourite

Creamy mashed potatoes mixed with spring onions are called champ in Ireland. This easy recipe combines a champ topping with a delicious savoury beef casserole.

Ingredients for 2

- 400g/14oz braising steak
- 1 tbsp sunflower oil
- 1 small onion, sliced
- 1 small clove garlic, peeled and crushed
- 15g/½oz plain flour
- 125ml/4fl oz dark stout
- 125ml/4fl oz beef stock
- 1 tsp tomato purée
- 215g/4oz button mushrooms
- 1 tsp Worcestershire sauce
- Salt
- Freshly ground black pepper
- 450g/1lb old potatoes, peeled and cut into chunks
- 2 spring onions, trimmed and finely chopped
- 7g/¼oz butter
- 1½ tbsp milk

Ingredients for 4

- 800g/1¾lb braising steak
- 2 tbsp sunflower oil
- 1 large onion, sliced
- 1 clove garlic, peeled and crushed
- 25g/1oz plain flour
- 225ml/8fl oz dark stout
- 150ml/¼pt beef stock
- 1 tbsp tomato purée
- 225g/8oz button mushrooms
- 1 tbsp Worcestershire sauce
- Salt
- Freshly ground black pepper
- 900g/2lb old potatoes, peeled and cut into chunks
- 4 spring onions, trimmed and finely chopped
- 15g/½oz butter
- 3 tbsp milk

1 Trim the meat of any fat or gristle and cut into neat cubes. Heat the oil in a large frying pan and fry the meat in batches until browned all over. Remove from the pan with a slotted spoon and place in a large heavy-based saucepan.

2 Add the onion and garlic to the pan and fry for 3-4 minutes until softened. Add the flour and stir until blended. Stir in the stout, beef stock, tomato purée and bring to the boil. Add the mushrooms, and season with Worcestershire sauce, salt and pepper.

3 Pour into the pan with the beef and stir well. Simmer, covered for about 1½ hours, until tender. Meanwhile, cook the potatoes in salted boiling water until soft then drain well.

4 Preheat the oven to 200°C/400°F/ gas mark 6. Mash the potatoes with the spring onions, butter and milk until fluffy. Place the braised meat and gravy in a large shallow heatproof dish. Spoon the topping over the top and fluff up with a fork. Bake for 15-20 minutes until the topping is light golden.

Tip

To freeze, cook the meat and topping and cool. Spoon the meat into the ovenproof dish and spoon over the cold potato. Cover with foil and freeze. Keeps for 3 months. To use, thaw for 2-3 hours then place the dish in a preheated oven 200°C/400°F/gas mark 6. Cook, covered with foil, for 20 minutes to heat the meat then remove foil and bake for a further 15 minutes to brown the topping.

Potato and Cabbage Bake

Family favourite

Potato bakes are always a popular family dish. Serve this one with grilled chops or sausages, or on its own as a complete supper dish. Use firm old potatoes such as Maris Piper.

Ingredients for 2

- ¼ savoy cabbage, washed
- 15g/½oz butter
- 50g/2oz streaky bacon, chopped
- 350g/12oz firm potatoes
- 75g/3oz Cheddar cheese, grated
- Salt
- White pepper

Ingredients for 4

- ½ savoy cabbage, washed
- 25g/1oz butter
- 100g/4oz streaky bacon, chopped
- 700g/1lb firm potatoes
- 175g/6oz Cheddar cheese, grated
- Salt
- White pepper

1 Preheat the oven to 200°C/400°F/gas mark 6. Finely shred the cabbage leaves and blanch in boiling water for 2 minutes, then rinse in cold water and drain well.

2 Heat the butter in a heavy-based pan and fry the bacon for 2 minutes until the fat runs and its starts to brown. Turn off the heat and toss the bacon with the cabbage.

3 Cut the potatoes into 6mm/¼in thick slices. Toss into the pan with the bacon and cabbage.

4 Arrange the potatoes, cabbage, bacon and grated cheese in a greased ovenproof baking dish, seasoning in between the layers with salt and white pepper. Pour over 3 (6) tablespoons of hot water. Cover with buttered greaseproof paper and bake for 30 minutes until the slices are tender when pierced with the point of a knife.

Tip

To freeze, cool in the baking dish and cover with foil. It will keep for 3 months. To use, thaw at room temperature, then reheat at 180°C/350°F/gas mark 4 for 20 minutes or until piping hot.

Mustard and New Potato Salad

Family favourite

The flavour of freshly dug new potatoes just cannot be beaten and this simple dish is great for a summer supper. It is also a useful standby for buffet parties if you need to feed any extra guests.

Ingredients for 2

450g/1lb new potatoes, scrubbed
225g/8oz pork chipolata or Frankfurter sausages
4 tbsp mayonnaise
2 tsp grainy French mustard
4 spring onions, trimmed
Ground paprika, to serve

Ingredients for 4

900g/2lb new potatoes, scrubbed
450g/1lb pork chipolata or Frankfurter sausages
8 tbsp mayonnaise
4 tsp grainy French mustard
8 spring onions, trimmed
Ground paprika, to serve

1 Place the potatoes, unpeeled, in salted boiling water and cook for 10 minutes or until tender. Test with the point of a sharp knife to see if they are done.

2 Meanwhile, grill the sausages under a hot grill until browned and cooked. Remove from the grill and slice thickly.

3 Blend the mayonnaise and mustard together in a large mixing bowl. Slice the spring onions into thin rings and add to the bowl.

4 If the potatoes are large, halve them to make evenly sized chunks. Add to the mayonnaise while still warm and stir in the cooked sliced sausages. Stir together and sprinkle with paprika. Serve warm or cold with a crunchy green salad.

Tip

Not suitable for freezing.

Spicy Pumpkin Soup

Freezer friendly

Growing the largest pumpkins can be a satisfying challenge, but you will have to use them all up in the late autumn! Make this pumpkin soup for Halloween, and keep a stock in the freezer to warm up the winter months.

Ingredients for 2

**500g/1lb 2oz pumpkin
  or squash
1 medium onion, peeled
25g/1oz butter
½ cinnamon stick
2 whole cloves
75ml/2½fl oz milk
Salt
Cayenne pepper
Soured cream, to serve
Chopped chives or bacon
  strips, to serve**

Ingredients for 4

**1 kg/2 ¼lb pumpkin
  or squash
1 large onion, peeled
50g/2oz butter
1 cinnamon stick
4 whole cloves
150ml/¼pt milk
Salt
Cayenne pepper
Soured cream, to serve
Chopped chives or bacon
  strips, to serve**

1 Peel the pumpkin or squash and scoop away the seeds and the fibrous middle. Chop the flesh into large cubes. Chop the onion finely. Melt the butter in a large pan and fry the onion for 1 minute.

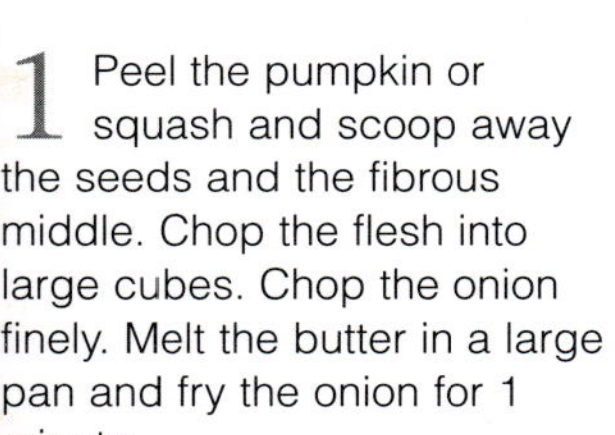

2 Place the pumpkin cubes in the pan with 225ml/8fl oz (450ml/¾pt) water and add the cinnamon stick. Stick the cloves into a piece of pumpkin.

Bring to the boil, cover then simmer gently for 30 minutes.

3 Remove the spices and purée the pumpkin in its cooking liquid in a processor or liquidiser.

4 Return to the pan and heat gently. Whisk in the milk and season with salt and a pinch of cayenne pepper. Serve with soured cream and chopped chives or bacon bits.

Tip

Freeze in freezer bags or boxes for up to 6 months. Thaw at room temperature or place in a saucepan and warm over a low heat.

Pumpkin Ravioli

Something special

Pumpkin-filled pasta served with butter-flavoured with sage leaves is served in the Tuscan region of Italy.

Ingredients for 2

150g/5oz strong bread flour
¼ tsp salt
2 small eggs, beaten
½ tsp olive oil
Fine semolina for dusting

Filling

250g/7oz pumpkin or squash, peeled, seeded and cubed
2 amaretti biscuits, crushed
½ tbsp white breadcrumbs
1 tsp pine nuts
½ small egg, beaten
¼ tsp nutmeg, freshly grated
1 tbsp Parmesan cheese, grated
½ tsp lemon zest, finely grated
40g/1½oz unsalted butter, to serve
2 sage leaves, to serve
Parmesan curls, to serve

Ingredients for 4

300g/10oz strong bread flour
½ tsp salt
3 medium eggs, beaten
1 tsp olive oil
Fine semolina for dusting

Filling

500g/1lb 2oz pumpkin or squash, peeled, seeded and cubed
3 amaretti biscuits, crushed
3 tbsp white breadcrumbs
1 tbsp pine nuts
1 small egg, beaten
½ tsp nutmeg, freshly grated
2 tbsp Parmesan cheese, grated
1 tsp lemon zest, finely grated
75g/3oz unsalted butter, to serve
4 sage leaves, to serve
Parmesan curls, to serve

1 Make the pasta dough. Sift the flour and salt into a bowl and make a well in the middle. Add the eggs and the oil. Work in the flour in a circular movement to make a soft dough. Knead for 10 minutes until smooth and elastic. Place in an oiled plastic bag and leave to rest for 30 minutes while you make the filling.

2 Heat the oven to 190°C/350°F/gas mark 5. Place the pumpkin or squash on a baking tray and roast for 30 minutes or until ttender. Cool, then mash or process with the remaining ingredients.

3 Divide the dough into two and roll each piece into two long thin strips. Continue to re-roll the pasta strips until they are thin.

4 Roll out two strips of equal length and width. Drop teaspoons of the filling about 7.5cm/3in apart on one strip of pasta. Brush round the filling with a little water and cover with the remaining pasta sheet. Press between the mounds to seal them and cut round with a pastry wheel or sharp knife to make about 12 (24) pieces.

5 Boil a large pan of salted water and cook the ravioli in batches for 2-3 minutes, draining well.

6 Melt the butter in a frying pan and add the sage leaves. Heat until sizzling but do not allow the butter to brown. Serve over the cooked drained ravioli with Parmesan cheese curls.

Tip

Freeze the raw, uncooked ravioli in layers interleaved with freezer film. They will keep for 3 months.

Squash and Celery Risotto

Vegetarian

Squash are easy to grow and you will get quite a few of these lovely orange vegetables from each plant. They are easy to store: just keep them dry and they will keep for many weeks.

Ingredients for 2

450g/1lb butternut squash
4 tsp olive oil
Salt
Freshly ground black pepper
1 tsp clear honey
2tsp sunflower oil
1 small onion, peeled and
    chopped
2 sticks celery, sliced
50g/4oz button mushrooms,
    sliced
2.5cm/1in piece fresh ginger,
    peeled and chopped
100g/4oz risotto rice
500ml/18fl oz vegetable stock
2 tsp lemon juice
1 tbsp flat-leaf parsley,
    chopped
Parmesan curls, to serve

Ingredients for 4

900g/2lb butternut squash
2 tbsp olive oil
Salt
Freshly ground black pepper
1 tsp clear honey
1 tbsp sunflower oil
1 onion, peeled and
    chopped
4 sticks celery, sliced
100g/4oz button mushrooms,
    sliced
5cm/2in piece fresh ginger,
    peeled and chopped
225g/8oz risotto rice
1l/1¾pt vegetable stock
1 tbsp lemon juice
1 tbsp flat-leaf parsley,
    chopped
Parmesan curls, to serve

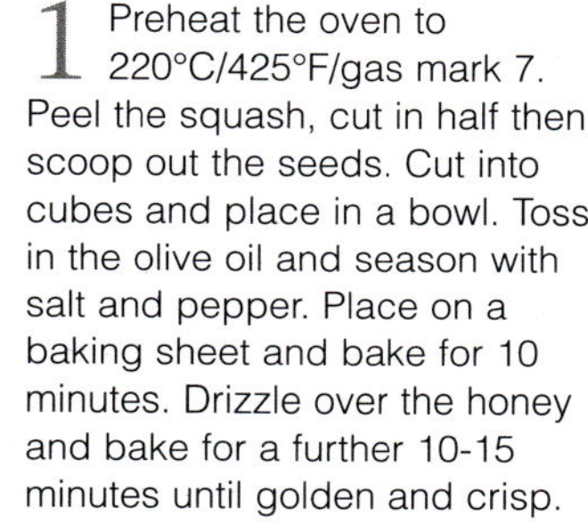

1 Preheat the oven to 220°C/425°F/gas mark 7. Peel the squash, cut in half then scoop out the seeds. Cut into cubes and place in a bowl. Toss in the olive oil and season with salt and pepper. Place on a baking sheet and bake for 10 minutes. Drizzle over the honey and bake for a further 10-15 minutes until golden and crisp.

2 Meanwhile, make the risotto. Heat the sunflower oil in a large deep pan or wok and add the onion, celery, mushrooms and ginger. Stir-fry for 2 minutes to slightly soften then add the rice and stir well.

3 Add a quarter of the stock. Stir well then simmer until the stock has been absorbed. Continue gradually adding the stock in batches until all the liquid has been absorbed.

4 When the rice is cooked, stir in the lemon juice. Add the roasted squash and stir together. Serve topped with chopped parsley and Parmesan.

Tip

Not suitable for freezing.

Braised Red Cabbage

Easy entertaining

If you grow red cabbage, you will find it stores well over the winter months in a cold garage or outhouse. It is worth cooking this delicious dish in bulk for the freezer and storing it in individual servings. Its velvety texture and sweet-and-sour flavour, make it ideal for serving with winter dishes such as roast pork or sausages.

Ingredients
Serves 4

800g/1¾lb red cabbage, trimmed and halved
1 tbsp butter
1 medium red onion, chopped
1 clove garlic, peeled and crushed

1 medium cooking apple peeled, cored and diced
2 tbsp cider vinegar
3 tbsp red wine
1 tbsp brown sugar
½ tsp salt
¼ tsp ground cloves
50g/2oz raisins
50g/2oz dried apricots, snipped

1 Place the flat side of each cabbage half on a chopping board and slice into thin shreds, cutting away the hard white core in the centre.

2 Melt the butter and fry the onion and garlic until tender. Add the cabbage and stir in the apple.

3 Add 90ml/3fl oz water and the vinegar, wine, sugar, salt, cloves and dried fruits.

4 Cover with a lid and simmer for 40-50 minutes until the cabbage is soft and tender. Serve with roast meats or Frankfurters.

Tip

To freeze, cook and cool, then freeze in strong freezer bags. It will keep for 6 months. To use, thaw at room temperature and gently reheat in a saucepan over a low heat or in the microwave on a medium setting, according to your manufacturer's instructions.

Pickled Red Cabbage

Store-cupboard special

Jars of spicy red cabbage look attractive arranged in your larder and are great to give as gifts around the festive season. Enjoy this crunchy pickle with cold meats all through the year.

Ingredients
Makes 1.5kg/3lb

1.5kg/3lb firm red cabbage, trimmed
175g/6oz salt
1.2l/2pt malt vinegar

1 stick cinnamon
10 whole cloves
1 piece blade mace
1 tbsp whole allspice
3 bay leaves
1 tbsp mixed pickling spice

1 Cut the cabbage into quarters then shred it finely, by hand or in a food processor, discarding the tough central core.

2 Layer the cabbage with the salt in a large non-metallic bowl and leave to stand for 24 hours.

3 Meanwhile, make the spiced vinegar. Place the vinegar, spices and herbs in a large pan, bring to the boil and simmer for 3 minutes. Remove from the heat, pour into a bowl and leave to infuse overnight.

4 Rinse the red cabbage well under cold running water and drain very well. Place in a bowl and strain the spiced vinegar over. Leave to stand for a further 24 hours, then pack into dry, sterilised jars (see page 20) and top up with vinegar. Cover with vinegar-proof tops, label and seal.

Tip

To store, keep the jars in a cool dry place away from daylight as this will alter the colour of the cabbage and make it become lighter.

Rich Pizza and Pasta Sauce

Freezer friendly

This sauce could not be easier to make and is the ideal way to use up a glut of tomatoes. Just add all the ingredients to one big pan and simmer them down to a delicious rich red sauce that you can enjoy all through the winter.

Ingredients
Makes 1.2l/2pt

2 tbsp olive oil
100g/4oz onions, peeled and finely chopped
2 cloves garlic, peeled and crushed
2 tbsp tomato purée

1kg/2lb ripe tomatoes, stalks removed
1 tbsp dried oregano
2 tbsp fresh basil, chopped
1 bay leaf
25g/1oz caster sugar
2 teaspoons salt
Freshly ground black pepper

1 Heat the oil in a large heavy-based saucepan and fry the onions and garlic over a gentle heat until soft and transparent, about 8 minutes.

2 Wash and drain the tomatoes, chop roughly and add to the pan with the tomato purée. Stir well then add the herbs and seasonings.

3 Simmer gently, stirring occasionally, for 30-40 minutes until the sauce has become a soft pulp.

4 Use the sauce straight away on cooked pasta or cool and pack into freezer bags or boxes to make individual portions.

Tip

Freeze in strong freezer bags or boxes and store in the freezer for up to one year. To use, thaw for 2 hours at room temperature and reheat gently in a pan.

Green Tomato Chutney

Store-cupboard special

If you have a glut of green tomatoes late in the year, do not worry. Tomatoes picked while they are still green have a dense texture and acid flavour that is ideal for making chutney.

Ingredients
Makes 1.80kg/4lb

1.80kg/4lb green tomatoes, roughly chopped
8 spring onions, chopped
4 green chillies, seeded and finely chopped

8 tsp ground coriander
2 tsp salt
Freshly ground black pepper
450g/1lb granulated sugar
600ml/1pt distilled pickling malt vinegar

1 Mix the tomatoes, spring onions, chillies, coriander and salt and pepper together in a large, non-metallic bowl, and leave to stand overnight.

2 Place the sugar and vinegar in a large pan and heat gently to dissolve every grain of sugar.

3 Add the tomato mixture and stir well. Simmer for 40-50 minutes or until the mixture is very thick. If the tomatoes are very large or hard, the chutney will take longer to soften down and become thick.

4 Ladle the chutney into warmed, sterilised jars (see page 20), cover with waxed discs, wax side down while still hot. When cool, cover with cellophane or cling wrap tops, seal and label. For the best flavour, store for 6 weeks before opening. It will keep for 1 year.

Roasted Tomato and Red Pepper Soup

Easy entertaining

This refreshing summer soup is easy to make ahead of time for a supper party and can be served hot or chilled. Roasting the vegetables in the oven retains the intense flavour in the tomatoes, making this truly delicious starter.

Ingredients for 4

700g/1½lb plum tomatoes on the stems, washed
2 red peppers, halved and cored
1 large red onion, peeled
1 large strip of orange zest
2 tbsp olive oil
400ml/ ¾pt vegetable stock
Salt
Freshly ground black pepper
Chives, snipped, to serve

1 Preheat the oven to 190°C/375°F/gas mark 5. Leave the tomatoes on the stems and place them in the roasting tin. Add the peppers and quartered onions with the orange zest.

2 Drizzle over the olive oil and toss the vegetables to coat lightly. Bake for 30 minutes or until the vegetables are soft and beginning to brown.

3 Remove the tray from the oven and leave to cool for 5 minutes. Remove the tomato stalks and then place contents of the pan in a food processor in two or three batches and blend to a purée.

4 Pour the purée into a sieve set over a large saucepan. Press the purée through the sieve into the pan then blend in the stock. Taste and season the soup with salt and pepper. Either heat the soup gently and serve, or chill and serve cold garnished with snipped chives.

Tip

To freeze, cook, chill and pour into freezer bags or boxes. It will keep for 6 months. To use, thaw at room temperature and taste the seasoning before use.

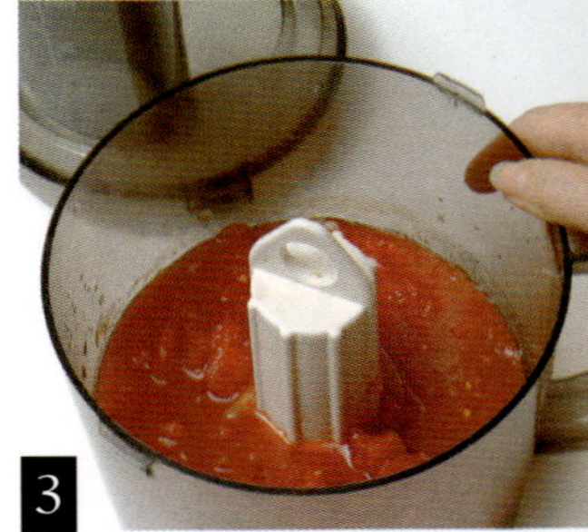

Winter Minestrone Soup

Freezer friendly

This hearty main-meal soup uses up a variety of winter root vegetables. If you do not have the exact ones to hand you can easily vary this recipe and if you want to make a vegetarian version, just omit the bacon.

Ingredients for 2

1 tbsp olive oil
25g/1oz smoked pancetta or
   streaky bacon, rinded
   and chopped
1 medium onion, chopped
1 small clove garlic, peeled
   and crushed
1 stick celery, diced
1 small turnip, peeled and
   diced
1 large carrot, diced
1 tsp plain flour
200g/7oz can chopped
   tomatoes in juice
750ml/1pt vegetable stock
1 medium potato, peeled
   and diced
50g/2oz Savoy cabbage,
   finely sliced
25g/1oz frozen peas or
   sliced beans
25g/1oz penne pasta,
   optional
175g/6oz can cannellini
   beans, drained
Salt
Freshly ground black pepper
Parmesan cheese,
   grated, and crusty bread
   to serve

Ingredients for 4

2 tbsp olive oil
50g/2oz smoked pancetta or
   streaky bacon, rinded
   and chopped
1 large onion, chopped
1 clove garlic, peeled
   and crushed
2 sticks celery, diced
2 small turnips, peeled and
   diced
2 large carrots, diced
1 tbsp plain flour
400g/14oz can chopped
   tomatoes in juice
1.5l/2 ½pt vegetable stock
1 large potato, peeled
   and diced
100g/4oz Savoy cabbage,
   finely sliced
50g/2oz frozen peas or
   sliced beans
50g/2oz penne pasta,
   optional
350g/12oz can cannellini
   beans, drained
Salt
Freshly ground black pepper
Parmesan cheese,
   grated, and crusty bread
   to serve

1 Heat the oil in a large, heavy-based pan and fry the pancetta until the fat runs, about 2 minutes. Add the onion, garlic and celery and cook for 3-4 minutes to soften slightly.

2 Add the turnips and carrots and stir for 2 minutes then sprinkle in the flour and cook, stirring for a minute to coat the vegetable cubes. Add the tomatoes and stock and stir well. Bring the heat up to just below boiling and stir until slightly thickened.

3 Add the diced potato, cover with a lid and simmer for 30 minutes. Add the cabbage and peas, raise the heat, then simmer for a further 10 minutes, covered.

4 Add the pasta and beans and cook for 10-15 minutes until the pasta is tender. Taste the soup and season with salt and freshly ground black pepper. Serve with grated Parmesan cheese and crusty bread.

Tip

To freeze, cook to the end of step 3 and cool the soup, without adding the pasta and beans. Pour into freezer bags or boxes and store for up to 3 months. To use, thaw the base for 2 hours, and cook from step 4.

Roasted Roots with Braised Beef

Easy entertaining

Everyone loves roasted potatoes, but you will find that adding more root vegetables to the roasting dish is even more delicious. This winter dish is a great served with melt-in-the-mouth braised beef.

Ingredients for 2	Ingredients for 4
500g/1lb 2oz piece silverside of beef	1kg/2 ¼lb piece silverside of beef
1 bouquet garni	1 bouquet garni
220g/ ½lb potatoes, peeled, cubed and parboiled	450g/1lb potatoes, peeled, cubed and parboiled
2 medium parsnips, peeled and quartered	4 medium parsnips, peeled and quartered
4 small onions or shallots, peeled and halved	8 small onions or shallots, peeled and halved
220g/½lb carrots, trimmed and scrubbed	450g/1lb carrots, trimmed and scrubbed
2 sticks of celery, trimmed	4 sticks of celery, trimmed
1 tbsp sunflower oil	2 tbsp sunflower oil
Salt	Salt
2 tbsp creamed horseradish sauce	4 tbsp creamed horseradish sauce
1 tbsp whole-grain mustard	2 tbsp whole-grain mustard
1 tsp cornflour	1 tbsp cornflour
150ml/¼pt beef stock	300ml/½pt beef stock
2 tbsp red wine	4 tbsp red wine

1 Place the beef in a deep heatproof saucepan or casserole dish and cover it with water. Add the bouquet garni and bring the water to the boil.

2 Lower the heat to a simmer, cover with a lid or foil and simmer gently for 2 hours. Place the potatoes and parsnips in a large pan of salted boiling water and parboil for 5 minutes. Drain well.

3 Preheat the oven to 200°C/400°F/gas mark 6. Place all the prepared vegetables in a roasting tray and toss in the oil. Season with salt. Place the tray in the oven and bake for 35-40 minutes until the vegetables are tender and have a dark golden tinge to their edges. Place on a warmed serving platter.

4 Drain the beef and place on a warmed platter. Place the roasted vegetables round it and keep it hot in the oven. Mix the horseradish and mustard with the cornflour and blend to a paste with 2 tbsp beef stock. Blend with the remaining stock and pour into a small pan. Heat until thickened, then add red wine. Spoon a little over the hot meat and serve the remainder in a jug. Serve the beef sliced with the vegetables.

index

credits & acknowledgements

Many thanks to Lakeland Plastics Ltd (www.lakelandlimited.co.uk) for supplying china for photography and to the photographer Colin Bowling.